S0-ADQ-746

ENCOUNTERSWITHGOD

rue Stories of Teens on a Sacred Journey

All Scripture quotations, unless otherwise indicated, are taken from the HOLY BIBLE, NEW INTERNATIONAL VERSION®. NIV®. Copyright © 1973, 1978, 1984 by International Bible Society. Used by permission of Zondervan Publishing House. All rights reserved.

Cover and inside design by Scott Ryan
Typesetting by Ahaa! Design
Cover and interior photos by David Strasser
Edited by Dale Reeves and Lynn Lusby Pratt

Library of Congress Cataloging-in-Publication Data:
    Encounters with God : true stories of teens on a sacred journey / compiled by Kelly Carr.
        p. cm.
Includes bibliographical references and index.
    ISBN 0-7847-1767-2 (pbk.)
1. Christian teenagers—Religious life. I. Carr, Kelly, 1977–
BV4531.3.E53 2005
248.8'3—dc22   2005006031

refuge™ is a trademark of Standard Publishing
© 2005 by Standard Publishing
All rights reserved.
Printed in the United States of America.

Standard Publishing, Cincinnati, Ohio.
A division of Standex International Corporation.

12   11   10   09   08   07   06   05

7   6   5   4   3   2   1

ISBN: 0-7847-1767-2

ENCOUNTERS**WITH**GOD

rue Stories of Teens on a Sacred Journey

Compiled by Kelly Carr

refuge™

an imprint of
Standard Publishing
www.rfgbooks.com

Thanks to Steve—the coolest husband in the world. God has used you to inspire me in many ways and to make me laugh on our journey together. Thanks Mom and Dad for believing in me and for always being there to cheer me on. And thanks to my friends and family who have encouraged me and have been excited with me as I put this book together.

CONTENTS

A MAJOR INTERSECTION

A PLACE TO REST

INTRODUCTION

You get that feeling inside when you're ready to go. What will you see? Who will you meet? More importantly, what should you pack?! So you find someone who's been there before and ask a ton of questions.

This book was put together to help you on the most important journey you'll ever take—your journey with God. But first, here are a few things you might want to know:

Why this book?

As the editor of ENCOUNTER—*The Magazine*, I've gotten to read hundreds and hundreds of stories from people about their relationships with Jesus. There are many I read and think, *That's just what I'm going through*! I want you to have that same chance to read their stories and learn from their spiritual experiences.

Who wrote the stories?

There are several types of authors you'll find in these pages:

- Most are teens just like yourself, dealing with family, friends and God, trying to make sense of it all. Several have also shared poems expressing their feelings about what it was like to learn from the Holy Spirit in these times of their lives.
- Some are adults who want to tell you things that happened to them as teens so you can hear how they made it through with their faith intact.
- And finally, some are Christian music artists. They want to share journeys from their teen years as well. They want you to see that they don't deserve to be lifted up on pedestals or be seen as any greater than you are. They haven't arrived—they mess up and struggle along the way just like you do.

How should I read it?

That's up to you. You can read it from cover to cover. You'll notice the stories are laid out in a way that takes you on the path of a journey in five sections:

- *Section one* covers the beginnings of people's journeys when they first met God or first decided to truly live for him.
- *Section two* shares stories about what people learned about themselves as they continued on in their relationships with Jesus.
- *Section three* is filled with big problems, the times tragedies hit people's lives and what they learned from those experiences.
- *Section four* includes stories on the mission field and other places of service where people put aside their own desires and reached out to others with the love of God.
- *Section five* has testimonies by people who are maturing in their relationships with Jesus and eager to grow more in him.

You can also read the stories by topic. Check out the index in the back of the book and pick out the ones that currently relate to you.

God has placed us on this earth to connect with one another. We don't travel this journey of life all by ourselves—we were made to help each other along and figure out who God is and what he's all about. So grab your stuff and let's go! Join the writers in this book for some incredible encounters with God.

—KLC

"Go in peace. Your journey has the LORD's approval."

—Judges 18:6

A PASSAGE
NOT YET TAKEN

"I had no direction in life. I was wandering aimlessly. Then suddenly I saw a passageway. After a few steps in, I felt an urge—something tugging me to keep going. So I started out to see what I'd find."

by Cindy L. Ooms

LEARNING TO TRUST 24/7

As I write this, my family is contemplating yet another move.

Have you ever thought that you had your life, or part of it, figured out? I have—many times!

Right now I know that every Wednesday afternoon I'll hear my band director's laugh as we fight through another challenging song. Every Wednesday evening I'll spend an hour planning our youth group's future and laughing at our pastor's antics. But all that can change in a moment; it has before!

Constant Changes

I've lived in eight cities and five states. Each time my family has been faced with another move, I've told God that I have a better idea—staying put!

What if we can't find another church that will help me grow as I have here? What if I can't find a friend I trust enough to tell my hopes and dreams? What if I never again hear my director laugh at our musical endeavors? Yet whenever I look back over my time in a location, I thank God for giving me the chance to meet so many awesome people and participate in so many incredible opportunities.

As I write this, my family is contemplating yet another move. Again I'm begging God to let us stay where we are. After all, eventually I have to settle somewhere! But haven't all the past changes taught me anything? When will I learn to trust him? Can't I see that he'll continue to care for me?

I'm certainly not alone in my fears. Even after a year of living 24/7 with the Son of God, the disciples had their doubts too.

Doubtful Followers

If you read Matthew 14:15-21, you'll see that the disciples couldn't figure out how Jesus was going to feed thousands of people. Wait a sec! Only a few chapters before this, we read that Jesus healed a man from leprosy, two men from demon-possession, and one man from paralysis; he even brought a girl back to life!

Jesus entered the scene with impressive credentials. Yet his disciples thought they had a better plan for the people's hunger—send them away. They acted as if Jesus would bring people back to life yet not care enough to make sure they were fed! Hadn't they figured out that Jesus thought only of others, not himself? His compassion is evident through his many sacrifices, whether denying himself sleep, meals or time alone to teach his followers and meet their needs.

Many times I have the same problem as the disciples. I enter every trial with the same doubt-filled attitude, forgetting everything God's already proved himself to be. When my granny had leukemia, he provided healing. During every move my family has made, he's provided comfort in my loneliness. For every doubt, he's provided stability. So why don't I trust him?

Bright Promises

One of my favorite Scriptures is Exodus 15:2: "The LORD is my strength and my song; he has become my salvation." Not only does God promise to give us the courage and power we need, but he also promises to plant a song in our hearts.

Another favorite verse of mine is Jeremiah 29:11: "'For I know the plans I have for you,' declares the LORD, 'plans to prosper you and not to harm you, plans to give you hope and a future.'" God doesn't just tell us he's planning a future for us; he also guarantees hope. He's not going to hand out a bleak, dismal future, but one bright with promise. He will provide!

Even when we aren't asking for God's help, he's giving it!

One of the greatest aspects of God's being our provider is his compassion. He doesn't just show up when times get tough, and he doesn't hold us at arm's length. Instead, he puts himself right next to us. He carries us when we can't walk on our own. Even when we aren't asking for his help, he's giving it! When we aren't crying at his feet, he's still fulfilling our every need.

When will I learn? When can I finally surrender full control of me and tell God that I trust him with everything—every day of my life? Because that's exactly what he wants.

Will I stay or move? I don't know. I can't guarantee anything in life. But I know someone who can, and I am learning to trust him . . . 24/7.

by Jeanette Hanscome

THE FAITHFUL ONE?

How many more wild parties did they expect me to clean up after?

I felt sure I'd done the right thing by telling Mom and Dad what my sisters were up to the last few times all three of us had been trusted to stay alone overnight. How many more wild parties did Sherry and Kristy expect me to clean up after, just in time for our unsuspecting parents to return from a weekend trip?

My parents were pretty upset but appreciated my coming to them about it.

Sherry and Kristy responded a little differently.

Totally Innocent?

"See if we ever trust you again," Kristy told me.

Sherry scowled. "I love the way you made us look like delinquents and made yourself look totally innocent."

I tried to defend myself. "Hey, Mom and Dad are mad at me too for covering up for you so many times."

"Poor baby."

Before walking out of my bedroom, Kristy informed

me, "Sherry and I are grounded. And we're probably back to having Grandma and Grandpa stay with us whenever Mom and Dad leave town. Real fun."

Sherry stayed in my room and just stared at me for a minute.

I hated having to feel like a snitch, a betrayer, just for telling our parents the truth.

"Not everything you do says 'I'm a Christian.'"

"Sherry, I can't keep lying to Mom and Dad so that you can party. We're supposed to be a Christian family, remember? You and Kristy don't act like it anymore. Look at the friends you hang around with, the way they're rubbing off on you. Mom and Dad don't know half of it."

My sister's mouth dropped open. "Oh, and what about you? Not everything you do says 'I'm a Christian.' And you still have Mom and Dad convinced that you're Little Miss Perfect."

What *About* Me?

Sherry got up and left me alone, with her last statement hovering in the air over my head. What *about* me?

I would be lying if I said that right then and there I sank to my knees in confession: "God, please forgive me. I am just as bad as my sisters, only better at hiding it." Instead, angry tears stung my eyes. How could Sherry say such a thing? My life looked a lot more Christian than hers did.

But for the next few days, I could not get Sherry's words out of my head. My mind was flooded with pictures, reminding me of times in the not so distant past when I had acted like anything but a daughter who respected her parents' standards when they were not around. Worse yet, my actions didn't show a faithful heart for Christ.

What was my real reason behind going to Mom and Dad about my sisters in the first place? Deep down I knew my biggest fear had been that our parents might learn about one of those weekend parties and bust all three of us. Better to confess on my own and choose the least self-incriminating version of the story possible. That way I got to look like the obedient, concerned daughter who would rather risk having her sisters disown her forever than see them go down the road to ruin.

Who's Looking?

I took great satisfaction in nailing Sherry and Kristy on their new choices in friends because none were Christians and most drank or smoked, among other things. But so did some of the kids I hung out with. My friends from the drama club and speech team weren't exactly a spiritual group. It didn't take much time with them for me to start using their language (never around Mom and Dad, of course) and enjoying things that pretty much killed my chances of being a Christ-like example.

What was my real reason behind going to Mom and Dad about my sisters in the first place?

Suddenly I flashed back to a time after a speech tournament when a bunch of us from the speech and debate teams got together. A girl named Natalie had a bottle of vodka and started passing it around the group. When the bottle was passed to me, I figured that everyone in the group, knowing that I was a Christian, expected me to pass it on. So instead, I took a drink and enjoyed the reactions on my teammates' faces.

Also my last two boyfriends hadn't been Christians, and I couldn't say that my behavior with them always pleased God.

"God, I have been such a fake."

So Sherry had me. I'd managed to look like the obedient, faithful one next to my sisters, but when nobody was looking, my life was saying, "I'm a Christian" less and less often. And as I had so smugly told Sherry, Mom and Dad did not know half of it.

Willing to Change?

"God, I have been such a fake," I confessed. I felt him speaking to my heart then, gently warning me that it would take more than admitting it. If I wanted to remain truly faithful to him, I needed to turn some things around, and fast. Was I willing, even if it meant leaving certain people and activities behind? It would be hard, but I knew that I could not go any other way.

Now I am grateful for the wake-up call brought on by the confrontation with my sisters.

I admit it's still difficult to stay faithful to Christ and to always make the best choices. Recently God had to convict me again—this time on my selection of books and movies. They definitely did not reveal a heart that wanted to serve and follow him. But like before, giving them up was worth pleasing Christ and living as one of the faithful.

The Hug of Grace

"For it is by grace you have been saved, through faith—and this not from your-selves, it is the gift of God" (Ephesians 2:8).

The worst feeling in the world is knowing that you've let someone down. There is a certain agony in the waiting—standing by, powerless, as a per-son decides whether or not he will forgive you. The feeling multiplies because you know you don't deserve forgiveness.

I betrayed a close friend of mine not long ago. I didn't tell him, but instead waited, hoping he would never find out. I sort of knew that he eventually would. He did discover my dishonesty shortly thereafter, and he confronted me. All the excuses I had stored up were suddenly useless. There were no words that could remedy the damage I had done to our friendship and to his trust.

One day that friend came to me and gave me a hug. He told me that he had decided to forgive me. He said he cared about me too much to let me go because of one mistake. His forgiveness felt great, but it also made me feel guilty. It seemed too easy, too quick, and definitely undeserved.

What I experienced is called grace, and it's God's gift to us. God loves us dearly; we are his most prized possessions. We take his love for granted daily and betray him with a constant stream of sin and deceit. The best part is, he still loves us. He certainly don't deserve it, but he gives us forgiveness anyway. He not only moves on, but he forgets our sins just as soon as he forgives them.

Grace is a hard thing to grasp, but just think of it as God's make-up hug.

by Lori Wootten (written at age 17)

by Sarah Hatfield

MY MIRROR, MY PRISON

My ribs and collarbones were painfully visible, the skin stretched tight over my cheekbones.

As I started getting ready for school one morning, I happened to glance in the mirror at myself, and I noticed with a certain twinge of disgust that I had started putting on a little weight. I didn't really think too much of it at the time, just that little feeling of distaste in my stomach.

Lost My Appetite

The next morning I looked at myself in the mirror again, this time longer and harder. It seemed as if in one day's time I'd gained fifteen pounds. It wasn't true, but that's what I could've sworn I saw. Later that day I was eating lunch with my friends, and I suddenly lost my appetite. The turkey and cheese sandwich I held in my hand began to smell and taste awful. I couldn't finish it, so I threw it away with the rest of my lunch.

The following day my reflection in the mirror looked about as attractive as that turkey sandwich. At breakfast, my cereal tasted like cardboard soaked in the rain. And I didn't even touch my lunch. I just tossed it into the garbage.

Each day things got worse. I started lying to my friends about why I skipped my lunch all the time. Then I had to start lying to my parents. I was never hungry anymore, and if I did feel hungry, I took that as a sign of success that I was losing weight. When I looked at myself in the mirror, my ribs and collarbones were painfully visible, the skin stretched tight over my cheekbones. I thought that I had never looked better!

Found My Worth

By then I was into my fifth month of full-blown anorexia. I skipped as many meals as I could. I even told my parents that every Thursday I was going to fast and pray so I could get away with skipping an entire day's worth of food.

It was on one of those Thursdays that I was reading my Bible, and I came across Psalm 139:14: "I praise you because I am fearfully and wonderfully made; your works are wonderful, I know that full well."

This verse sparked a change in my life. I was already a Christian and thankfully under God's grace. But I finally began to see my worth as a child of his and the beauty that he had given me.

It's still a daily struggle to get up in the morning and feel OK about myself. But I have found a deeper level of God's love, and I'm moving one day at a time in his miraculous grace.

ONE WAY

RELIENT K | MATT HOOPES

WHAT I BELIEVE

*I was really being challenged to
define my faith.*

I shifted in my desk chair, replaying the assignment
in my head. The professor said we had to write whether
or not we thought Jesus was the Messiah, based on the
Old Testament. It would be an interesting project, one
that would take some research. I was up for it, though.
The subject fascinated me and I wanted to dig deeper.

Church Upbringing

I was officially a senior in high school, but I was taking a few classes at a local Christian college to finish up my last year of schooling. Between this Old Testament class and an oral history class, I was really being challenged to define my faith.

What made my religion the right one?

I'd grown up in a Christian home. My mom worked at our church as a children's pastor, and my dad was an elder. It seemed whenever the doors to church were open, my family was there. I loved church and had a great upbringing.

In junior high I started playing the trumpet, and then later on I learned to play guitar. I really enjoyed music.

A Guitar and a Band

I started listening to the radio a lot in junior high. My mom had a guitar and I'd pick it up. She taught me to play a couple of chords on it. I decided to learn to play songs I was hearing on the radio, like ones by Hootie and the Blowfish and things like that. I really felt attached to the guitar, and I just wanted to practice all the time.

In high school, I got together with my friends Matt Thiessen and Brian Pittman. We all went to church together. We started out doing praise and worship during youth group. Matt had written some of his own songs, so eventually we started doing shows and named ourselves Relient K, in honor of my first car.

When we got our record contract, they encouraged us to graduate high school early so we could go on tour. We did, but the tour was delayed. So instead, I signed up for some classes at a local Christian college.

The One True Religion?

As I dug into my latest assignment, I realized that Buddhism, Islam and Judaism all had similarities to Christianity. What made my religion the right one? Other people of different faiths were as sincere about their beliefs as I was of mine. Could I be sure that Christianity was the one true religion?

I started a quest to make my faith my own. I didn't want to believe something just because my parents did. I wanted to believe it because it was true. I read books, talked to people I looked up to and prayed to God for wisdom in discerning all the information I'd learned.

I still have to work to keep my faith fresh and relevant.

By the time I turned in my paper, I knew that Jesus could be proved the Messiah of the Old Testament. I had no doubts that the Bible was true, that Jesus was Lord and that Christianity was the real thing. My faith had been renewed.

Out on Tour

Eventually, Relient K did go on tour. God has blessed us immensely as a band, and I feel so fortunate to do what we do. I feel so honored to play the guitar for a living. I love music, and I love doing this and getting to meet people. I realize that not everyone gets this opportunity. It's like being at summer camp, only it's all the time.

I still have to work to keep my faith fresh and relevant. There are things that sometimes block me or distract me. It's somehow easier to mess around on the Internet or play a video game than it is to read my Bible. That doesn't change when you're on the road.

But I know God is real and that Christianity is true. I'm glad I was able to stand on my own two feet and make my faith my own. I now know without a doubt that the God we sing about is the one true God of the universe.

by Elisha Petersen

CONFESSIONS OF A SUNDAY MORNING CHRISTIAN

I went to church every Sunday with my family, but that was the extent of my relationship with God.

Strobe lights illuminated the room while the DJ played yet another great jam. It was a typical Saturday night. Stumbling teenagers gyrated against one another, beers in hand. I overheard some kid across the room say to his friend, "Doesn't that girl over there have church tomorrow? She's such a hypocrite, just as all Christians are."

Living Two Lives

There are obstacles in each of our lives that we are forced to face every day. How we deal with those obstacles strongly affects others around us in ways we cannot always see.

"The greatest single cause of atheism in the world today is Christians, who acknowledge Jesus with their lips, then walk out the door and deny him by their lifestyles. That is what an unbelieving world simply finds unbelievable." That powerful statement by Brennan Manning should be a challenge to all of us as believers.

When I was in high school, I considered myself a Christian, but I was not really following God—I did what I wanted, when I wanted. I went to church every Sunday with my family, but that was the extent of my relationship with God.

Though my friends knew I considered myself a Christian, they could not see any difference between themselves and me. I was what some people call a Sunday morning Christian. I would party and drink with my friends on the weekends and then go to church Sunday mornings. I never imagined the extent to which this type of behavior would hinder me in the future.

Ruined Reputation

During my senior year of high school, I rededicated my life to Christ. I finally realized how wrong I had been before, and I wanted to live in a way that was pleasing to God. I stopped drinking, got involved in youth groups and Bible studies and tried my best to set a good example for others.

But my witness was ruined before it even started. When I shared with my friends the reasons I stopped drinking, they thought I was trying to act like I was better than they were. They would just respond, "You have no right to tell us that drinking is wrong when you used to drink with us." They thought I was judging them when really I was just trying to love them.

I never imagined that because of my former behavior, my credibility would be destroyed. It really hurt me, but I had no other choice than to accept it and try to keep living as an example.

As sad as that was for me, it taught me a lot. I am now much more conscious of my actions. I know I have to live consistently with what I claim to believe.

Second Chance

Because I have stayed strong in following God over the past few years, people have begun to notice. My friends are now starting to see that my relationship with God is real. Some of them have asked to talk to me about my faith. One friend even gave her life to Christ as a result of our discussions. I never would have thought that I could have a part in something like that.

Because of my former behavior, my credibility was destroyed.

It is amazing the ways God works in our lives. He wants us to be examples of him. We can affect so many people's lives just by living out what we believe.

Always be aware of your actions. Do not be the reason that someone else does not know Jesus. But remember that even if you do mess up, God will forgive you if you ask. He can still use you in unimaginable ways to further his kingdom.

No One

Oh, I once thought that I was loved,
but now I see that down this road,
no one understands who I am,
because . . .

No one ever knows how I feel inside

No one ever sees the clear tears I sigh

I could scream at the top of my lungs,
and no one would hear my cries

I could be yelling all day, and no one
would look me in the eye

No one ever knows . . .

No one ever sees . . .

No one ever hears . . .

No one ever looks . . .

But then I saw this new road,
and at the end of it I saw him.

He approached me silently,

He touched my cheek and said,

But I love you.

I said, God is that You? I wondered when
You'd come.

My life's so confusing without You.
I mean . . .

No one ever knows how I feel inside
No one ever sees the clear tears I sigh
I could scream at the top of my lungs,
and no one would hear my cries
I could be yelling all day, and no one
would look me in the eye

No one

No one ever knows . . .

No one ever sees . . .

No one ever hears . . .

No one ever looks . . .

No one

No one

No one

No one

No one ever knows how I feel inside

No one ever sees the clear tears I sigh

I could scream at the top of my lungs,
and no one would hear my cries

I could be yelling all day, and no one
would look . . . me . . . in . . . the . . . eye

"Don't think that I'm the only one who
loves you

your family and your friends love you
too.

Just know that I'll be with you again,
very soon. . . ."

by Jenna LaValle (written at age 12)

by Jennifer Dunning

A LIFE CHANGED IN TEN SECONDS

I hoped that I would die painlessly.

Most of us don't realize how quickly our lives can change forever. My life changed quickly one night as I sat watching movies with my family.

The Ride of My Life

The sky was an unimaginable display of color as a thunderstorm rolled in. Our movie watching stopped suddenly when we lost power. Then our discussion of plans for an evening without electricity came to a halt as my parents yelled for us to head for the front hallway.

I obeyed in confusion and found myself sprawled onto the floor for the ride of my life. I felt our house leave the ground. I heard my mother scream amid the roar of something terrible. I shut my eyes tightly and hoped that I would die painlessly. I was sure the time had come for me to meet my Lord.

The Lord had a different plan. When I opened my eyes, there was still a floor underneath me. My family and I had survived the tornado without a scratch. Our home, on the other hand, was destroyed. As I stood in the rain and stared at what used to be my house, I began to weep for those who had no place to call home. I knew then how they felt.

No Place to Call Home

My brother and I moved from southern Indiana to Pittsburgh, where we spent the summer with my biological father, stepmother, and two brothers whom we barely knew. This felt as far away from home as possible.

I waited the entire summer for news from home. Would we be building a new house or moving? Where would I have to start school? When could I see my family? When could I visit my friends? I just wanted my life back!

The end of the summer did not bring an end to my misery. We still had to wait for a while before our new house was built. So, back near Indiana, I moved in with my grandmother while the rest of my family lived in a small apartment across town. Starting eighth grade in a new school was the hardest part. I refused to make new friends, convinced that I would be there for only a few weeks. Those few weeks turned into several lonely months.

Finally, it came time to go home—to a new house! One of the greatest times of my life was returning home to realize how much I had been blessed. It had taken ten seconds to take it all away, and as God slowly gave it back to me, he taught me so much.

I realized how little I had thanked him for all I had. I learned firsthand that people who are hurting need compassion. Life had a whole new perspective. I was determined to live and use all I had to serve God. After all, he had given me everything, and he could take it all away in ten seconds!

by Quinn Rowkoski

THE HYPOCRISY TRAP

We were devastated. Our youth leader had betrayed us.

When I was in middle school and early high school, my church had the coolest youth group in town. Teenagers from churches without youth groups or churches with inactive youth groups joined ours, as well as teenagers who didn't go to any church at all.

A Growing Group

Part of the reason those of us who had been around for a while liked to keep going back was because of the church's excellent outreach and spiritual growth opportunities. Every Wednesday we had praise and worship and Bible study. We went on a lot of missions trips, and we planned a lot of Christian events at our public school. Part of the reason that new people came to youth group was because of our fun events. Every Sunday we had game nights, and we had a lot of fun outings like ice skating, hayrides and bonfires.

The biggest reason that all of us liked youth group, however, was because of our awesome youth group leader. He was young, energetic, fun and compassionate. All of us looked up to him as a spiritual leader and role model. He was a good friend, and some of us even saw him as a father figure.

One of my friends, Kim, particularly looked up to our youth group leader as a father figure. I had known Kim since elementary school, and I knew she was hurt that her father had left her and her mother when she was just a baby. I wanted her to know about our Father in Heaven, so I invited her to youth group. She soon came regularly, and through our youth leader's influence and the other youth group members' outreach, she also became a Christian. She, like the rest of us, learned a lot about the Bible and had a lot of fun at youth group, largely because of our youth leader's leadership.

One Shocking Moment

Everything seemed perfect, and then our youth group leader did something that shocked everyone. One Wednesday we went to Bible study, and he did not show up. We waited around for a while, thinking he would come late, but he never came at all. Instead, the church secretary came and told us that he would not be arriving that night and would probably not be our youth leader anymore. We went home confused and upset.

A few nights later, there was a meeting with us and our parents at which we were told what had happened. Our youth leader had left his wife and three young daughters for an eighteen-year-old sponsor of our youth group.

This news was devastating to all of us. We struggled to understand why our youth leader, who we thought was so godly and influential, would do such a thing. We became angrier and angrier at him.

Kim took the news particularly hard. She was not there the night we got the news, and I had to go to her house to tell her what had happened. As I stood on her stoop and rang her doorbell, I remember feeling angrier than ever at our former leader for betraying us all in such a way, and especially for betraying Kim, who had trusted him so much. Why did I have to tell my friend, who had become a Christian largely because of his influence, that this man had done such a thing?

When I told her about it, she said, "My own father left me, and [our leader] felt almost like my father. And now he left us too. I never thought this would happen to me twice."

> **We did not want to ever be the reason that someone else did not believe in God.**

After this, I felt angry, not only at the youth leader but also at God. Why would God give us such a great person, knowing that he would end up sinning in such a way?

In Whom Do We Trust?

I still don't have all the answers today. I wish that the story had a happier ending—maybe that our youth leader had realized his wrong and asked us to forgive him. This isn't the case. He and his girlfriend left the church and, as far as I know, are still together.

So many times I hear people give a popular reason for not being a Christian: all the Christians they know are hypocrites. We now understood—many of us for the first time—the reason a lot of nonbelievers don't believe.

If there is a lesson that our youth group learned from our youth leader's sin, it was that we were hurt by hypocrisy. We saw a Christian not only sin but also fall a long way down from his respected position. I am sure everyone in the youth group asked the same things I did: How could we trust any Christian when we had trusted one who seemed so strong and then hurt us and God so much? How could we know whom to really trust and look up to?

There is an even bigger lesson that we eventually learned from the experience though. We eventually realized it was not God who let us down—it was our youth leader. God would be willing to forgive him as soon as he wanted forgiveness. We could not let his sin cause us to lose faith in God, or we would only be sinning as well.

Seeing the Trap

The one good thing that came out of the tragedy is that we understood the hypocrisy trap. We became determined to live lives of integrity and not hypocrisy. We did not want to use our youth leader as a reason not to believe in God, and we did not want to ever be the reason someone else did not believe in God.

Maybe someone you once looked up to let you down and made you wonder if anyone could ever be a trust-worthy Christian. If so, you know how it feels, and you know that you can't perpetuate the problem. Don't let another person lead you away from God. Be determined not to fall into the hypocrisy trap so that when others see you consistently living a life of integrity, they will be led closer to God.

Open Arms

I have stumbled; I have fallen
I have gone far astray
I am that lost sheep
Falling further every day

It is so different, Lord,
Without you in my life
Instead of finding love and kindness
I find anger, hate and strife

Lord, I am miserable
I realize what I lack
But I have done so much wrong
Will you ever take me back?

Yet you welcomed me with open arms
Now I've ceased to roam
You pulled me into your embrace
And whispered, "Child, welcome home."

by Lauren Wulfhorst (written at age 15)

MORE THAN
A MIDDLE SISTER

I shook my head, terrified at the thought.

We were about to start the first leg of our tour as Out of Eden. I roamed around backstage, biding my time until we were up. I always got a case of flutters before performing, wondering if anything would go wrong or if I'd flub up. Thankfully, my sisters did most of the talking, so I just had to worry about singing.

"Andrea, you're going to have to do the altar call."

I snapped my head toward my sister's scratchy voice. What in the world was she talking about? "Excuse me?" I asked, desperately hoping that I'd heard her wrong.

When you have siblings, you get put into a box.

"I'm losing my voice," Lisa said, touching her throat. "I need you to offer an invitation."

I shook my head, terrified at the thought. My palms had already begun sweating at the mere mention of it. "I can't do it."

My older sister laid a hand on my shoulder. "You're going to do great. Just be yourself."

She sounded so confident, but I wasn't sure. My sisters were much better at these things than I was. They were always the popular ones. I, on the other hand, was the middle sister.

Comparing Myself

My entire life I'd struggled with comparing myself to my sisters. When you have siblings, you get put into a box. People are like, "This is how she is; this is how you are; this is how you compare. She's better at this; you're not." There's a lot of that when you grow up with sisters.

My oldest sister Lisa was super popular in high school. She ran for class president and prom queen. Danielle was also very popular, but in a different way. She had this wild, crazy thing going on, and everybody knew who Danielle was.

I, on the other hand, was really shy. I knew everybody, but I didn't really care too much for the whole high school experience. I loved studying. I enjoyed schoolwork and all that. I didn't really invest in a lot of relationships. The whole experience seemed a little trivial, so I just did my thing and had my friends but didn't do too much socializing.

Sibling rivalry was definitely a real thing in my life. It was hard to appreciate the differences between my sisters and me and to simply focus on what God had for me. I thought I would outgrow it, but in high school it was still going strong.

I have to admit, comparing myself to others wasn't limited to my sisters. I would look at other people to compare myself. I would want to be better than they were. That's so awful! I struggled with being content with what God had me doing and where God had me. It was hard for me not to look at other people.

My Turn to Talk

Stage techs rushing around backstage pulled me back to reality. We were ushered onstage and our concert started. The entire time I had flutters in my stomach as I anticipated doing the altar call. As the end of the concert neared, the butterflies only became worse. I knew I had to trust God in order to get through this.

God had used me right where I was.

But God, Lisa is so much better at this than I am. Even Danielle would do a better job. They're more outgoing. I'm not a speaker! I'm more of a background person, not the frontman. How am I going to do this?

Inevitably, the concert wound down. I stepped forward and prayed God would use my words. They flowed with surprising ease. I didn't sound like Lisa or say the things she might have said, but it worked. God had used me right where I was, as Andrea Kimmey, and it hadn't flopped.

After that experience, I knew I had to stand on my own two feet and learn to appreciate what *I* had to offer, not compare myself with everyone else. We finished our tour, and I went back to high school for my junior year.

Who I Am

For some reason, it felt so much easier to deal with the pressures of high school after that first tour as Out of Eden. Slowly my concern over what other people thought of me disappeared. I felt some of my comparison problem easing. I wasn't afraid for people to know I was a Christian, nor was I afraid for people to know that I sang and that God was using me. The burden of caring was gone.

I felt some of my comparison problem easing.

Just stepping out in faith helped me to realize that God had given me so many awesome abilities and talents and gifts—I didn't have time to compare myself to others. I have enough abilities in myself that I don't have to worry about what he's given other people—I only need to appreciate others, not compare myself.

When you compare yourself to others, you lose who you are because you're constantly going, "Well, maybe this is how I am" or "Maybe this is who I'm supposed to be." You become all these things to all people to seem perfect, but then you don't even know who are you. It's better to just find out who God made you to be and be that consistently. Comparing yourself to others is exhausting.

I've really had to realize that God has created us differently for different reasons. In the past I've looked at my sisters and at Out of Eden and said, "You know, they're so good at speaking" or "They're so good at this." I would feel like, why am I here? I didn't understand. I wanted to be in the background and let them do what they were good at.

It's better to just find out who God made you to be and be that consistently.

It wasn't until I stopped comparing myself to them that I found my strength and what God called me to do in Out of Eden. He made me to be just the person he wanted, and I didn't have to worry about how I measured up to others. I just had to focus on being everything I could be.

by Natalie Bedell

WE ALL MAKE MISTAKES—MINE WAS BEING NORMAL

I sat there watching people from school getting high and drunk.

Another day of high school, and I arrived at the front steps. I was definitely your average teenager. I always had someone to hang out with, and I was always the one being asked to hang out. I had everything I wanted, right? Well, that's where the plot thickens.

Choices to Make

We all know the daily peer pressures that come with being a teenager. I admit, some of those pressures I irresponsibly fell into. I found myself at parties, hanging out with people I had known all of my life, but things had changed. Now, instead of playing tag and worrying about who was going to be "it," we worry about what to tell our parents of our whereabouts.

We had unknowingly grown up. We had become teenagers. Now we have choices to make.

I have to say that I never really got into the party scene and would usually be on the side hanging out. But still, I sat there watching people from school getting high and drunk. The worst part was that I began to be immune to it. No longer was I the one preaching about how lame it was to get wasted. I was the one sitting there laughing at my drunken friends' jokes. What had come over me?

Hooked on the Lord

Then my brother Jason obtained an internship at a local church and invited me to go. I saw nothing wrong with that and decided to give it a try. I went, and I loved it right away. I eventually got involved, singing in the praise band and attending every youth trip that became available.

I am hooked on the Lord. I have changed for the better, and so have my friends. We attend church every Sunday now, and we can't get enough. Instead of finding an outlet for our problems, we've turned to the best answer of all—God.

by Rebekah Jordan

OUT OF THE DARKNESS, INTO HIS LIGHT

The only way I could force myself to sleep was by taking sleeping pills every night.

Why, God? Why me? What did I ever do to deserve this?
Have you ever found yourself asking God these questions? I have, many times. Sometimes I even get angry with him and wonder why I go through hard times when I'm following him. The truth I need to constantly be reminded of is that God is not here to magically remove the trials and struggles from our lives but to help us through them and to make us stronger people because of them.

Falling Apart

When I was fifteen, I was convinced that my life was falling apart. I had always been happy and emotionally stable, but the summer before my sophomore year, I fell into a sudden depression and started having panic attacks. I worried about everything, and the only way I could force myself to sleep was by taking sleeping pills every night. It wasn't long before the pills stopped working. I spent countless nights crying in the dark, watching the red numbers on the clock flash into midnight, then 3:00 AM and then dawn.

Those were the scariest feelings I had ever had because I was no longer in control of anything, not even myself. I couldn't make decisions—not even the simplest ones, such as what to eat. I couldn't concentrate on anything. It would take me hours to do ordinary things, such as putting on my makeup or cleaning my room. I would sit at my desk all afternoon trying to finish some easy five-sentence grammar assignment.

When shopping, I felt lost and helpless unless my mom was right by my side, helping me focus and telling me what to do. I felt so pathetic, but I would literally freak out unless someone was there, guiding me step-by-step through whatever I was doing.

The panic attacks were the worst. My heart would race and pound really fast, and my thoughts would run wild. There was nothing I could do except breathe deeply and wait until they were over.

Depending on Medicine

Finally I let my mom drag me to the doctor. I knew there was something wrong with me, but I didn't want to go because I didn't want to hear it—almost as if a diagnosis would make it all seem so serious and eternal. The doctor gave me medications for depression, anxiety and insomnia.

I was amazed at how one little pill could bring me that sweet, deep sleep I had been craving for so long. At first, the medicine was a lifesaver, and then it became an addiction as I felt too afraid to stop using it.

I felt trapped. I had finally reached the point where things were starting to improve, but it was all due to a couple of pills. Underneath all the drugs I was still the same weak person. I depended on the medicine to cover up that other self instead of dealing with it.

Trusting God's Strength

That's when God brought an amazing psychologist into my life, and I started going to counseling sessions. That was the ultimate turning point because she helped me deal with issues I had tried to forget. She opened my eyes to the hope in my "hopeless" situation. She encouraged me and guided me in my relationship with God.

With the psychologist's help, and by starting to depend on God's strength, I slowly reduced the dosages of all my medications. One morning I woke up and realized I had slept through the night without any medicine, and that was the day my spirit felt renewed again.

Underneath all the drugs I was still the same weak person.

The healing process took a while, but I owe it all to God. I see the lesson he was trying to teach me all along was to depend on him for everything and not to rely on myself. He wants to be my Father, my counselor, and my friend, not just a distant creator. Now that it's over, I can see how God's hand was on everything, helping me grow.

Opening My Eyes

I look back on my struggles, and I see a totally different person from who I am today. It amazes me how God works. He has the power to transform people from being weak, sick, insecure and vulnerable to strong, happy, confident and mature. I just had to accept that his timing is perfect and that he knew what he was doing.

God uses the toughest times to mold us into the people he wants us to be.

I realize that God uses the toughest times to mold us into the people he wants us to be. Today I look at any problems I face with a new attitude and a different perspective because of what I went through and what God showed me. I'm even hoping to be a counselor someday so I can help people the same way my psychologist helped me.

"So we fix our eyes not on what is seen, but on what is unseen. For what is seen is temporary, but what is unseen is eternal" (2 Corinthians 4:18). The unseen things in my life, those things I was so blind to, are the things I am most thankful for today. Those unseen things drew me closer to God and taught me so much.

God's plans are so much greater than we could ever comprehend, and that is why he deserves complete control of our lives. Even through the pain and the suffering, he is doing wonderful things in our hearts. If we are patient and don't give up, we will come through into the light, and those unseen things will be revealed to us.

AN UNEXPECTED DISCOVERY

"I've been on my way for a while now, and I'm realizing something strange. I started out trying to explore what was going on around me, but I'm finding out more about what's inside me. There's a strength I've never known. I feel like I'll be different somehow just because I'm taking this journey."

by Caleb Hicks

THE BEST AND WORST OF BECOMING A MAN

In retrospect I wish I'd had someone to sit down and talk with me about what was going on.

I am at a very significant time in my life right now, at the transition of crossing over from boyish adolescence to manhood. No one can tell me when I have become a man. Only I will know when I have truly crossed over.

I have no prior experience—as this only happens once; yet I anticipate what is to come. I want to explore the best and worst of this transition.

Changes

My early childhood is hard to recall perfectly and accurately. I was happy while my parents were together. Tragically, they fell out of love with each other and divorced. I was six when they divorced and didn't understand it at all. Even now, at sixteen, I still don't understand it. Both remarried within a year or so, and I was the middle child in both families. At too young an age, I closed myself off from the rest of the world.

Physically, becoming a man is awkward. Anyone who's gone through the changes of puberty can tell you that. From growth spurts to a changed voice to hair in odd places—I went through it. All of the sixth grade girls made fun of my voice and the other boys' voices cracking every three or four sentences. The fact that the girls were about a foot taller than all of the boys at this time didn't help things too much.

When these changes began to occur, I kept what I could a secret for as long as possible. It was embarrassing to me. In retrospect, I wish I'd had someone to sit down and talk with me about what was going on, even if it was awkward and embarrassing. It was something I wished I didn't have to go through by myself. But I have a security in my identity that I could have gained only from going through these things alone, despite my regret for not confiding in someone.

Growth

I made my share of mistakes. When I was fourteen, I experimented with two very deadly things that I shouldn't have. Alcohol was the first. I saw some adults in my life do it, so I didn't see the harm in doing it myself. I was wrong. Marijuana was the second bad choice. For about four months I smoked it every chance I could, and I regret it every day.

My parents found out about the marijuana, and I was grounded for six months. During that time I went to the only place that I was allowed to go socially: church. I found new friends in my youth group, and a whole new world opened to me. In that time I went to a youth convention where I rededicated my life to Christ.

I've grown so much physically, mentally and spiritually in two short years. I've given my life wholly to God, and he is molding me into the man that I am to become. I've come to realize that all I have that is good in my life comes from him. He's already made me to be all he wants me to be. Now I just have to grow into it.

The closer I come to manhood, the more I realize my own imperfections and faults.

It is reassuring that, as long as I give my life to God, I will never be more or less of a man than he wants me to be. The most maturing and the most growing that I've done has been in him. I will trust him always.

Journey

This world is still a bad place, full of evil, turmoil, strife and sin. To know that I come from a humanity that has failed God a billion times over is devastating. The closer I come to manhood, the more I realize my own imperfections and faults. I understand and accept that I am incapable of doing anything good on my own, because I linger in a realm of sin, waiting for my Savior to rescue me.

The best thing is waking up every day and realizing how much beauty God has hidden in the people of this world. He made mankind fearfully and wonderfully in his image. We all are special poems printed in the palms of his hands. I realize how little I can accomplish by myself. That's OK though—God can do phenomenal things through me if I open myself to his will.

I'm not a man now, but I will be soon. I don't know exactly when. Yet I know God will show me in due time because he is faithful.

Despite the strife I've endured, I've somehow grown to love this journey I'm making. It's only because I have a God who turned my life around. I found happiness in him, and I am so amazed at how much he loves me. When I look at this life and think that the best is yet to come, I smile and turn my face to the heavens and give praise.

by Elizabeth Westra

WHY ME, GOD?

My body was attacking itself—my immune system turned on my own body.

When he told me, I just sat there like a dope and stared at him. *What did he say? He can't be talking to me.* When I didn't move or speak, Dr. Borck repeated, "Did you hear me? You have lupus."

I just sat there. Mom started crying. I didn't feel anything then. It took me hours before it all sank in.

My body was attacking itself—my immune system turned on my own body. It mostly hits women, something about our hormones. All that day I wandered the house in a daze. I kept thinking, *It can't be. That's for older people. Why me, God? What have I done?*

Then I was on tons of drugs. A long, thin, tan pill for the rash, a yellow one for pain, a blue one to keep the others from eating my stomach, and one or two more. I hated taking pills. I wasn't sick.

And there was the "moon face" side effect—when my face puffed up like a blowfish. It was all from one of the medicines. I skipped it for a while, but then I got worse and Mom yelled at me. She did that a lot. "Did you take your medicine? You know how tired you get—don't overdo it—blah, blah, blah," like I was a kid. She was always edgy.

Then Dad—he acted weird too, all cheerful and hearty. I think they called it denial. "Hey, how's my girl?" he'd say. "Here's something I brought you—a little surprise." Then he'd hand me candy or flowers. It made me feel like I was dying or something. Well, I wasn't. I wasn't even sick.

Friends?

And my friends? What friends? Stacy, my best friend, acted friendly, but she smiled and gushed too much.

"Hey, how are you? Uh, I mean, you look great. Want to go watch Mitch at practice? Can you walk that far? You don't have to be so grouchy. I didn't know."

Then I thought she was avoiding me. The other kids stared like I was a circus freak. I saw them whispering and looking at me like maybe they thought I had AIDS or something. They were probably saying stuff about me like, "What's wrong with her? Look at her face—all puffed up. I'll bet she's just getting fat."

I got used to avoiding everyone. It was just easier to duck into the restroom than face their fake smiles.

But what hurt the most was how Mitch acted. At first he was like usual—a little concerned but still teasing and funny. Then, when my face got all puffy and blotchy, he acted different—kind of stiff and formal. He stopped coming to my locker and started just nodding in the hall. I wanted to yell, "Hey, it's still me! I'm no different!" What made me mad was that he never once asked me about it, never asked how I really was inside. I could have used a friend then—a real friend.

That's when I met Tara at a support group.

Support

Mom and Dad didn't want me to go to the support group at first. "Your health can't take it," Mom said. "You start going out at night and you'll get sick again."

"You don't need that," Dad said. "You're not like them. You're just a little sick." Well, I went anyway, and I'm glad I did. There were mostly grown-ups there—women about Mom's age. But there were some girls my age. I wasn't the only moon face.

I wanted to yell, "Hey it's still me! I'm no different!" I could've used a real friend then.

At first I sat in the back and tried to duck out before anyone could talk to me. Then this girl with wild red hair and a strong chin marched up to me and said, "Hey, how come you're running away? We don't bite." She was great. She made me laugh, and we even helped each other with makeup tips to cover the rashes.

Tara said I didn't have to handle it alone. She said she'd help me, but God would help too. That kind of surprised me. I blamed him for letting me get sick. Tara said that God doesn't make people sick. Illness comes because there's sin in the world, but God can use me for something beautiful anyway. She said maybe God will use me to help other girls with lupus. I never looked at it like that. Maybe Tara and I could help others together.

That wall I built around myself to keep everyone out—it's cracking. Thanks to God and Tara. I talk to kids at school again. Some kids even ask me about lupus. The other day I told my science class about it. People even asked how it affected my life. I told them the truth. Some even stayed behind to talk. Most of them weren't avoiding me. They just didn't know what was wrong and were too embarrassed to ask. And Mitch? Well, I think it's over with him.

Anyway, now I can admit without crying that I have lupus, and I'm learning to live with it. I have help.

ADMISSIO

OOC1

*591
51.6

Who Am I?

I look in the mirror and wonder . . .
Who am I?

Am I more than my reflection
So shallow and finite?

Am I more than the clothes I wear
So temporary and irrelevant?

Who am I
When darkness comes and I search
for light?

Who am I
When friends forget to call and I
am alone?

Who am I?

Will I ever know the answer?

Or is the journey of searching

The quest of faith I am to take?

by Hope Fillingim (written at age 14)

by Cherith Long

UNDER FIRE

Mr. Tyler's bitter words were like bullets, and I was being bombarded.

My new geography teacher was a pot-bellied man with skinny legs. With his white beard and thin hair combed over a balding head, he reminded me a bit of Santa Claus. Until he began to teach.

Mr. Tyler's Beliefs

Mr. Tyler was an atheist—he made that abundantly clear. He talked like a New Ager, encouraging us to get good karma, as well as emphasizing his own extreme environmentalist, pro-choice, what's-really-wrong-with-assisted-suicide views. His bitter words were like bullets, and I was being bombarded.

By the end of the first class, my stomach was in knots. I was so upset I almost felt nauseated. As I stumbled to my next class, I wondered how I would survive the semester.

I prayed hard before the next geography class. *God, please give me wisdom,* I begged. *Let me know if I should say anything.*

Things got worse. Mr. Tyler told crude jokes, encouraging the students to be immoral. *Most of these people are non-Christians,* I thought. *They don't need more encouragement to sin.*

My stomach clenched, and my blood boiled. But I didn't know what to say.

When students raised their hands to ask questions, Mr. Tyler's sarcasm came through. "Didn't you hear me the first time? You want me to spend the whole class time repeating myself?"

So I kept my mouth shut—and prayed under my breath whenever I had the chance. It made me so frustrated. I couldn't very well argue with the teacher in class. And it wouldn't help to go to the principal, since Mr. Tyler tied all of his outrageous views into his teaching. Geography has a lot to do with culture and religion—I just hated the parts that Mr. Tyler chose to teach.

I kept praying—and sitting through class with my mouth shut. I knew God had compassion for Mr. Tyler, but all I felt was anger.

Not Another Hypocrite

Finally, during one class, Mr. Tyler made an offhand comment about his mom who had Alzheimer's. For a moment, his usually cold, piercing blue eyes glassed over, and I felt a sudden flicker of understanding. Mr. Tyler wasn't a true atheist. I believe he was actually furious with God, wondering how a loving God could allow his mom to suffer.

After class, I gathered my courage and asked Mr. Tyler if he had ever gone to church. In his usually bitter manner, Mr. Tyler told me how his parents had dragged him to church every Sunday when he was young. "Just a bunch of little do-gooders," he sneered. "There comes a time when you have to face reality." He thought of Christians as unrealistic and hypocritical.

I smiled, told him a bit about my background and why I was a Christian, and then told him I'd pray for him.

Mr. Tyler laughed and made some crack about, "Yeah, a guy like me really needs some prayer." But I could tell he was touched.

I gathered my courage and asked Mr. Tyler if he had ever gone to church.

For the rest of the semester, I sat through geography class. As with all my classes, I committed to studying hard. Despite Mr. Tyler's off-the-wall comments, I showed interest in his teaching and spoke up when he asked the class questions. I didn't cheat and didn't fudge on assignments. Mr. Tyler thought Christians were hypocrites, but with me he wouldn't have that excuse.

When it came time for a group project, I chose a partner who was more known for his goofing off than his intelligence. Mr. Tyler raised his eyebrow and asked me more than once why I'd pair up with a loser like that. Well, he didn't use the exact word *loser*, but that's definitely what he meant. I just smiled and said we were doing fine—I'd make sure the guy did his part.

My Changed Attitude

By the end of the semester, my attitude toward Mr. Tyler had changed. Although I was still occasionally disgusted by his sarcastic comments and anti-Christian ideals, I felt mainly compassion. On the last day of class, I again told Mr. Tyler I was praying for him.

I'd love to tell you that Mr. Tyler chose then and there to become a Christian. But he didn't. The verse, "One sows and another reaps" (John 4:37) is true in this case.

With God's help, I had chosen to love Mr. Tyler. I had chosen to be respectful, to study hard and to help my classmates whenever I could. I may not have seen a dramatic transformation in Mr. Tyler, but he couldn't scoff anymore that Christians were hypocrites with no integrity.

I knew I had planted some good seeds. Now it was up to God to make them grow.

by Elizabeth Lehman

REVERSING THE ROLES

It is hard to be the parent for my own parent.

As I sat in the waiting room, I flipped nervously through a magazine. I couldn't even concentrate on the photos or the titles of the articles. I looked around the room filled with women of various ages, and I knew they were all there for the same reason. It was the same reason I was here with my mom.

After what seemed like hours, my mom's name was called, and we slowly followed the nurse down the long corridor to another room. As we waited again, my mom sat on the patient's table while I sat in the chair placed in the corner.

Our roles had changed. Now I had to be the strong one. I smiled, although I wanted to cry. I said it would be OK when I was not really sure it would be.

Diagnosed with Cancer

That day, my mom was diagnosed with breast cancer. Cancer has always been a part of my life. Three of my grandparents died from cancer. My one surviving grandmother was diagnosed with breast cancer around the same time that my mom was diagnosed. Miraculously, my grandmother's cancer was determined to be a false alarm. But my mother's cancer was and is real.

Due to the cancer, my mom had surgery and chemotherapy treatments. As such, she is unable to continue her normally busy schedule. She cannot work because the chemotherapy makes her too sick to move. Now I act as the parent. I have to cook the meals, clean the house, wash the laundry, go grocery shopping and care for my younger brother and sister.

Ironically, I enjoy these activities and do them without complaining. It is, however, a struggle to know that I have to do them because my mom is too sick to do them herself. It is hard to be the parent for my own parent, especially since I am only twenty-one and barely an adult myself.

Learning to Trust

I often wonder why this happened to my family. When I start to doubt or feel despair about any situation, especially concerning my mom's cancer, I remember Romans 5:2-5:

"And we rejoice in the hope of the glory of God. Not only so, but we also rejoice in our sufferings, because we know that suffering produces perseverance; perseverance, character; and character, hope. And hope does not disappoint us, because God has poured out his love into our hearts by the Holy Spirit, whom he has given us."

This is an important Scripture in my life because it

lets me know there is hope in every situation. No matter how hard it is to see at the time, I know that I can have hope in my Lord.

With great hesitation, I went back to college in the fall. My mom is three hours away, and now I am unable to help her. For me, this causes even more pain and frustration because I cannot be there to assist her. I want to be there and take care of everything, but I cannot. Instead, I must continue to trust the Lord and pray fervently for my mom.

My mom's cancer is still not completely eradicated. She is currently having new chemotherapy treatments. Despite this rough journey, I know the Lord is always there, and I simply must remember to trust.

by Mariesa Rang

FROM MY PERSPECTIVE

The Lord gave me 36 inches of height, and I will stand tall for him, every inch of the way.

Much about my life seems big. My dad is 6′ 6″. I get lost at crowded family gatherings. I'm a huge Chicago Cubs baseball fan. I wear bulky cowboy boots when I attend country music concerts. My career dreams rise into the clouds. And I hope a sizable state university is in my future.

Yet amid my large-scale lifestyle, I see the world from a smaller perspective. My parents say I'm one in a million, but it is actually closer to one in 30,000. What makes me exceptional? I am a dwarf.

Created for a Reason

When I was born, I arrived six weeks early and weighed less than 5 pounds. Within a few years, I recognized obvious physical differences between my friends and me. They rode their bikes to school. I needed a ride from my mom. At recess they ran around playing kickball and tag. I watched from my wheelchair. Sometimes kids picked on me for being little, but it rarely bothered me because they didn't understand my uniqueness.

Life isn't easy. Dwarfism comes with certain limitations. I finally started walking at four years of age. Numerous surgeries filled my early years. I used a trachea tube through fourth grade. I have a shunt in my head, and I drive a wheelchair at school because walking from class to class exhausts me. My parents remodeled parts of our home so I could reach light switches, tabletops, and sinks. In addition to my small stature, I have scoliosis.

Some people feel sorry for me, but it's not necessary. God created me for a reason.

I enjoy a unique perspective on life. On average, dwarves live a normal life span, but health complications constantly loom. Accepting this reality forces me to live life one day at a time and appreciate the little things (pun intended!). I never doubt why God made me this way and rarely wish that my life were different (except at amusement parks, since I'm not tall enough to ride roller coasters!).

Learning Life's Lessons

Life has ingrained into me a couple lessons that stand out. First, I do my best to treat others as I want to be treated. I don't see the Golden Rule as optional. I understand emotional pain. It hurts to walk into a restaurant and overhear children ask their parents what is wrong with the small person.

There is nothing wrong with me. I love chocolate chip cookies, movies, video games, and music, just like every other teenager. It bothers me when people assume that my brain and emotions are inferior just because I'm short. I'm a normal kid with normal interests. Therefore, I try to treat all my peers with respect.

The second lesson I've learned relates to God's perfect plan. In Psalm 139:13, 14, David writes, "For you created my inmost being; you knit me together in my mother's womb. I praise you because I am fearfully and wonderfully made; your works are wonderful."

I've decided to embrace the way God made me rather than chase after something I'm not.

I personally paraphrase the verse by stating, "God doesn't make junk!" The Lord gave me 36 inches of height, and I will stand tall for him, every inch of the way.

Obsessed with Image

I find it interesting how obsessed my peers can be with image. It's unfortunate that the power of one pimple can destroy an entire social agenda. For some, a bad hair day should be registered as a natural disaster.

I even know a friend who acted as if the world were over when cut from the basketball team. In life's grand scheme, not playing on the team isn't that big of a deal. At my size, being able to shoot the ball all the way to the rim would be a great accomplishment. Therefore, until my jump shot progresses, I've told my sports agent to market me to NBA scouts only as a point guard!

Don't get me wrong. I do my share of complaining, but I wish the world (including me) could stop focusing on what they don't have. Why are so many people preoccupied with changing what is already good? Americans drive nice cars, yet many want something faster. Beauty fills the world, yet stores can't stock enough beauty products. Every day, billions of people participate in physical activity but aren't happy unless they perform like an Olympic athlete.

I realized long ago that I won't be strutting down New York's or Milan's fashion runways anytime soon. So I've decided to spend my time embracing the way God made me rather than chasing after something I'm not.

Heading to the Future

As for my future, I'm in the process of qualifying for a driver's license. College is just around the corner, and I'll need to progress in various tasks of independence for that to become a reality.

In spite of an uncertain future, I stand on the promise that God is in control. I can't say I know what my purpose is just yet, but I am learning that life is more fulfilling when lived by faith.

In spite of an uncertain future, I stand on the promise that God is in control.

So much of what lies ahead falls outside of my control. My physical limitations prevent me from certain professions, and the thought of living alone is a bit scary. Fortunately, God has a way of working in major ways. He gives me an abundance of hope. My joy flows like a swollen river.

I'll travel wherever God sends me with the confidence that, although I'm small in stature, God has huge plans for my life.

ADMISSION

DOC10

*591
51.6

I Am From

I am from Kentucky

Born from a woman who gave me away

Still young and uncorrupted by the
outside world

I am from blazing summer days

And cool nights of story time

With the quiet laughter of trees like
tinkling bells

Blowing through my soul

I am from pencil and paper

I am the girl who writes but is
reluctant to share

Her dreams with the world

I am from bright colored ornaments

From family and friends

I am from music

The child of poetry, love and sin

I long to race with the angels

Across the broken sky

I am from Adam and Eve
Graced but with one great flaw
I am from people who love me
Even when I do not love myself
I am from the sun, the stars
I am the black rose from the holy
  grotto, waiting
For someone to come and bloom me into
Life
Still waiting

by Ellen E. C. Snell (written at age 13)

by Taylor D. Verner

GROWING UP

My mouth had to be wired shut for eighteen months, and my tongue was sewn down for two years.

Another day on the playground at recess was like being put on display for all the students to see. The steady laughter and pointing that came from the other students was enough to drive me mad. The constant, repetitive, annoying questions such as, "Why is your mouth like that?" "Does it hurt?" "Can I see?" "Why can't you play?" "Why do you eat that stuff?" And the worst: "Are you a freak?"

A Tumor

Growing up I had to go through eighteen reconstructive surgeries that started at age eight and ended at age fifteen. My problem is called an acute juvenile ossifying fibroma. There are only three known cases in the world, and my case is the only one in the United States. The tumor itself was very aggressive—it dissolved my chin bone and the floor of my mouth, leaving me with virtually nothing in my mouth.

When the tumor was removed, my bottom teeth were embedded within the tumor, and there was no way to salvage the teeth and attempt to replace them. The surgeries consisted of removing bone from both of my hips and my left rib to be put in my chin. My mouth had to be wired shut for eighteen months, and my tongue was sewn down for two years to make the floor of my mouth.

This caused me to have to eat blended up food. I was not able to play outside or play any contact sports, for my face might be hit and everything would be destroyed. It was too fragile.

I had to go through an awful lot for an eight-year-old. I was forced to make decisions on my own because my parents were not with me at school. The teachers did not fully understand what I was going through, so they decided not to try and see.

Yet there were a few people outside my family that I considered angels in my life. They would let me eat with them on some days, and on others, when they caught the other children misbehaving or acting rudely toward me, they would quickly put it to an end.

Shunned

"So what's on the menu today, Taylor? Slop? Barf? Brains? Or your favorite—guts?" teased a boy nearby. Eating lunch every day was the same routine. I would go in and sit down at the end of one of the lunch tables, trying not to make eye contact with anyone. Yet without fail, everyone surrounding my table would stop what they were doing to turn and look at my purple lunch box that had my name written on the front in big black letters, courtesy of my mother. They awaited the moment when I opened it.

I would sit there, pretending not to notice their stares that seemed almost to penetrate my very soul. I would proceed to open the lid, revealing a large syringe that had SpaghettiOs pasta, milkshakes, or anything else that could be put through a blender and squeezed through the little hole at the end. The children didn't care that my mouth was wired shut or that I didn't have a floor on the bottom of my mouth or that I didn't even have bottom teeth to chew with. All they saw was that I was "different" or, to them, a "freak."

Soon I found an easier way to eat. I would go late to lunch so I wouldn't have to pass anyone in the hall, and I would go to the girls' restroom, sit in the last stall on the very end and eat by myself in complete silence—something that was golden to me. People have asked me "How did you get through it?" All I can say is I was strong and as stubborn as I could be. That is what got me through.

> ## *I would go to the girls' restroom and eat by myself in complete silence.*

I never said anything back to the kids when they spoke, and I never made any bad gestures. All I did was look them in the eye so that maybe they could, for one second, see that I did have feelings and that I was a human being.

Not So Different

Accepting the fact that I was *not* so different was a little harder though. I had to realize that just because I wasn't able to play as many games outside, or eat the food the other children ate, didn't mean I was different as a human being. It only meant that physically I was incapable of doing those things.

This was hard for other people to understand too. I found that my real friends consisted of my family, other adults and a select few children who had good hearts and were able to see around the physical differences that I had.

Most of all, the one person who loved me and kept me safe and strong was the Lord. He helped me overcome all I had to face. I remember one day I said to my mother, "I don't understand why so many bad things happen in the world! If there is a God then why does he cause those things to happen?"

She replied, "He doesn't cause them to happen. He helps you overcome the pain and suffering you are feeling." I have always remembered her words.

As hard as it was, I tried to pick out the good in each situation. First, I found that there were not any other kids in my school who were in medical books by the age of eight. I was pretty special! Second, this whole situation was making me a stronger person. Last but not least, I realized how much my family, relatives, friends, and Jesus cared about me. I knew that I would always have them by my side.

Bridges to Cross

I went through my nineteenth surgery on December 17, 2002. They had to reconstruct my upper and lower jaw again. Everything came out better than we had expected. I now am able to say with a grateful heart that, because of the wonderful doctors who worked on me, I have a full chin and jaw line, and all my teeth rest gently upon one another.

Throughout my years at school, I taught myself how to be strong and not hate people for what they said and did to me. I learned how to accept myself the way I was. God had a reason for what I was going through. I learned that within every bad thing or every problem that might come along, something good would come out of it.

Everyone in life has difficulties to face. But when they're over, you can walk away knowing you made it and that you grew through it.

I realized how much my family, relatives, friends and Jesus cared about me.

I am hoping that someone somewhere out there will read this and realize that in life, there are bridges that have to be crossed—and in some instances, the bridges are rickety with a few boards missing here and there. You just have to try your best to make it around those hardships and obstacles. You can find the strength to do it in Jesus—he wants to help you get across.

SUPERCHIC[K] | MELISSA BROCK

SEARCHING FOR BEAUTY

I had to lose weight. There wasn't any other option.

"You've got chubby ankles."

My cheeks flamed. The guy I had a crush on had just announced one of my imperfections for anyone listening to hear. I wanted to hide, to bury myself under a rock and never come out.

Was it true? Did I have chubby ankles? Even worse, was I fat?

If he thought my ankles were chubby, everyone probably did, I figured. I could just see people talking about it at parties or in the locker room. "That Melissa Brock, have you seen her ankles? They're huge!"

Whatever the Cost

I decided at that moment that I had to be beautiful, whatever the cost. I began flipping through magazines, soaking in the perfect supermodels gracing the pages. I bet none of them had chubby ankles.

After staring at those picture-perfect faces, determination gripped me. I had to lose weight. There wasn't any other option. In order to be beautiful, I had to be skinny. To be skinny, I had to lose weight.

Their comments made me more determined than ever to keep losing weight.

I formulated a plan. I wasn't an exerciser, so that was out. But I could control what I ate. In fact, I just wouldn't eat for a while. I'd lose some weight and then reintroduce myself to food. I wouldn't let it get out of control. It would be like a fad diet, of sorts.

"You Look Great!"

I didn't waste any time putting my plan into action. Food became something from my past. Though the hunger pains overwhelmed me, it was worth the sacrifice. I convinced myself that this was the only way. After a while, the mere thought of food made me feel sick.

When I did eat, it was only to appease people, just so they wouldn't realize what I was doing. And even then,

I wasn't really eating. I'd move the food around on my plate, but only pretend to actually consume my meals.

I could always think of ways to excuse my not eating. I'd say, "Oh, I ate earlier" or "I'm just not feeling well today" or "I'm going to eat in just a little bit." There's always some excuse you can give to cover up the fact.

I got down to about 100 pounds in a few months.

People began telling me, "You look great!" and "Wow, you've been losing weight" and "What's your secret?" Their comments made me more determined than ever to keep losing weight. I was on my way, and happiness was right around the corner.

God's Creation

One day, I was chatting with my best friend. By the look in her eyes, I knew she had something serious on her mind. She sat down, opened her Bible and read Psalm 139:14, which said, "I praise you because I am fearfully and wonderfully made."

"You love God, right?" she asked.

What kind of question was that? I wondered. "Of course I love God," I told her.

"And you know God loves you, right?"

"Yes."

"What are some of the things in his creation you think are beautiful?"

I began naming oceans and mountains.

She looked me straight in the eye. "If you think all of those things are beautiful and God made them, then why can't you think you're beautiful, because God made you?"

Something clicked in my mind.

My friend had struggled with bulimia. She saw the signs that I was developing an eating disorder and was determined I wouldn't go down the same road she did. When I saw the concern in her eyes, the reality hit me of what I'd been doing to my body, the body that God created.

Inner Beauty

I realized I couldn't waste time trying to emulate the beauty I found in magazines or on TV. They portrayed a worldly kind of beauty, one that wouldn't last for eternity. A beauty that was going to make me happy, that was going to make me feel loved, was a kind I realized God had placed in me.

When I searched deep inside of myself, I realized I wasn't really happy, even after I'd lost weight. I'd assumed that people would like me more, that my life would be better. In reality, the same people who loved me before still loved me. Nothing had really changed except that I'd dropped some weight.

That's when the biggest turnaround started. I remember one morning looking in the mirror, and it was like God gave me a glimpse of myself through his eyes. He let me have one glimpse so I knew things were different than what I had imagined.

I realized I wasn't really happy, even after I'd lost weight.

After that day, I shared with several people that I had a problem. I counted on friends and family to keep me on top of things. I knew my struggle was too hard to conquer alone.

Wonderfully Made

It's been over a decade since that summer. Anorexia isn't something I just fought and it was over. It's something I deal with every day.

For me, there are times when everything is fine.

Then there are days when I wake up and feel ugly or fat. Those are the times when I have to ask for God's help. It is honestly a one-day-at-a-time thing, though it does get a bit easier. Every day that I've fought it off is another day that I've succeeded.

Every day that I've fought it off is another day that I've succeeded.

You know, I bet that guy I liked way back when never even realized how drastically his comment affected me. He probably doesn't realize that I'm just now finally getting to the place in life where I can let go and accept who I am in Christ. I now realize that Jesus has made me beautiful, despite what anyone else says. God created me in his image and I'm fearfully and wonderfully made.

One Little Miracle

It's one of those days.

Gloomy.

Overcast.

The sky a dark brooding blanket
suffocating me.

A Monday, naturally.

Back to school, back to work.

Back to reality
with all its daily stresses and tedious
rituals.

Sometimes it seems I spend all my time
on an endless list of tasks and
assignments

instead of doing anything worthwhile

anything worth mentioning

to anyone.

If I died tomorrow, would they have
anything to write

in my obituary?

My teacher says if you dread every Monday

that means you waste one-seventh of your entire life.

If you live seventy years

that means you spend ten whole years being unhappy.

For some reason

hearing that today

just makes me more depressed.

I am scared of death.

My greatest fear is wasting my life.

But sometimes it all seems so pointless . . .

Homework, tests, dentist's appointments, washing dishes

why do we even bother?

We only have a limited time on this earth.

Why do we spend it living a life we are bored with

doing things we don't want to do

being a slave to the conformist system of society?

Sometimes my life seems so meaningless
I just want to scream.
I mean, why am I here
just to be a follower?

I close my math book.
Put down my pencil.
Slip on my sandals.
Birkenstocks.
My dog Gar looks at me, curious
ears perked up hopefully.
I can never resist those begging eyes.
I go into the kitchen
return with his leash
fasten it on with a click
as he leaps around in circles
near bursting with excitement.
I wish I could be that content
and a simple ten-minute walk

could bring me so much joy.

We can learn a lot from dogs.

There is this path close by my house.
It runs beside a barranca and looks out
to the orchards.
Rows and rows and rows of leafy green
and fragrant orange blossoms in summer
and, in the distance, spidery branches of
trees
silhouetted against the sky.
It calms my soul, to walk along this
path.
Quiet except for the occasional chirping of
a bird
or Gar's loud exuberant sniffing.
But today, even the path seems dismal
the trees shiver in their stark cold
branches.
The orchard is silent
and the sky is dark and overbearing.

I sigh, walk along
my mind a web of sadness
as bleak as the boundless gray of the sky.
Then suddenly a ray of light
shines through the darkened gloom
to reveal white clouds and blue sky.
A patch of Heaven amidst a world of
desolation.
Heaven.
Is it a sign?
I pause and stare, transfixed.
Then suddenly, a jerk on the leash.
I stumble forward.
Gar, oblivious, his nose to the ground,
keeps pulling me along.
I am almost scared to look skyward
again
half-thinking it will be gone.
A vision, maybe.
A figment of my faith-craving
imagination.
So desperate for a little hope.

I slowly lift my eyes
a tiny peek.
And, yes! It is still there.
The same sunny ray shining through the
clouds
like a piece of Heaven, just for me.
My Heaven.
I smile.
One little miracle
and suddenly
my life is beautiful once again.

by Dallas Woodburn (written at age 17)

by Kim Peterson

TRUE TREASURE

Mom and Dad's fights drove us out of the house again.

Something skittered across my face and woke me from an already restless sleep. Grabbing at the creature, I surprised myself by catching the offender. I staggered up from the floor and flipped on the light. A roach! Ugh!

I flung it away and then decided I'd better squash it so it wouldn't bother me again. I woke my mother and little brother trying to kill it. Mom told me to forget it, soothed my brother and went back to sleep.

Not me! I was *not* sleeping on that floor again if bugs were going to join me.

Leaving Home

I sat upright and seethed with resentment. If my parents would just work out their problems, I wouldn't be stuck in this joint with bugs and who knew what else. I could be home in my own comfortable bed.

We did go home for a few days, but Mom and Dad's fights drove us out of the house again. For several months, I went to school in the morning from one refuge and often came home to find my possessions had been moved to another location—some nice, some not.

My parents eventually divorced, ruining my senior year of high school. What good things we would have had were squandered in their fights. Mom, my brother and I found ourselves on welfare and a few other government aid programs. My middle-class life disappeared.

I think my reaction to this crazy lifestyle was typical. I couldn't depend on home and people, so I latched onto the things that went with me. They were *mine*.

Finding Security

The Bible says a lot about our possessions, and most of the verses relate to our attitudes about what God has given us. Check out 2 Kings 5 and you'll see one example.

Gehazi had been hired to help Elisha. So he was present when Naaman, the commander of the king's army, went to Elisha for help. Naaman's skin disease was healed, and in his joy Naaman offered Elisha part of his wealth. The prophet turned it down, but Gehazi envied Naaman and felt he and the prophet had a right to be paid.

Gehazi followed the commander and requested money and clothing. Naaman gave willingly, but God punished Gehazi for his greediness. His attitude led to a bad choice.

Unlike Gehazi, I didn't wrestle with envying others for what they owned. I didn't crave riches and more possessions either. I already knew that loving money and things doesn't bring satisfaction. The temporary thrill is empty and short-lived (Ecclesiastes 5:10).

But because I wanted my life to be normal again, I did draw my security from what I owned. My stuff became unnaturally important to me because I could control these things when the rest of my life was falling apart.

I relied on clothes, stuffed animals, a few trinkets, books, a radio and more to comfort me and to make me feel safe. I tried to prevent damage to them as they were carted from place to place.

I could control these things when the rest of my life was falling apart.

I resented my parents, especially my mother, for touching and moving my things instead of letting me pack them. We often argued about this infringement. I was so wrapped up in my needs and possessions that I added to her troubles. I thought my attitude was protective, but I was selfish.

Transferring Trust

The rich man in the Gospel of Luke was blessed with much wealth. He decided to keep his abundance to himself and hoard it. But he didn't live to enjoy what he had saved (Luke 12:16-21).

I wasn't storing away lots of stuff, but like that man, I had made my belongings into my treasure. Fortunately, God slowly and gently helped me transfer my trust and taught me to rely on him. God wants me to treasure him; then the possessions he gives to me will be treated with the right attitude (Matthew 6:33).

I learned that people leave, things wear out and items that do last go out of style. Even tastes change. I can't count on these things. But God is constant, and his love for me is secure. I can count on him.

by Melissa Hill

A LESSON FROM THE GEESE

God just decided it was time to take more drastic measures to get my attention.

The other day God decided to teach me a lesson while I was sitting in traffic.

I was in a bad mood. I was angry. I'd shifted into runaway mode.

I thought, *I just have to get out of here. I have to go somewhere. Everything is driving me nuts.*

Running Away

So I was going to Target because I love Target. It's one of my favorite stores. Unfortunately, the Target closest to my house is on a very busy, over-developed area, which, of course, has more than its fair share of traffic. The cars were barely oozing down the road.

But I decided to use the extra time to go over in my mind (again) all the things that were bugging me, all the "grand injustices" I was facing. I was letting my anger and my frustration and my stubborn will run my thoughts. And I realized that at the bottom of all my violent emotions there was nothing—no real problems, no real crimes—nothing. Only restlessness and helplessness.

I was out of control, not only of the things that were going on around me, but even out of control of myself. I was completely powerless to change any of it. I didn't know why or what to do, and it just made me more mad.

Then God stepped in. Not that he wasn't there all along. He just decided it was time to take more drastic measures to get my attention. This particular time, for whatever reason, God thought it was best to use Canadian geese to get my attention. About fifty of them. All crossing this busy street.

Stopping to Wait

It was ridiculous, but I had to laugh. Here were five lanes packed full of cars, self-righteously trying to drive where we wanted to go as fast as we could. But then the geese decided to cross the street, in no particular hurry. And we had to sit and wait, completely out of control.

Now that I'd stopped and calmed down some, God seemed to whisper in my ear. *It's OK. Slow down and relax. You can't control your life, but I can. I'll take care of you, just trust me.*

And, of course, I already knew all that, but I'd sort of forgotten, sort of ignored it. But I decided to remember it—and keep remembering it.

And then immediately, really right at that moment in the traffic with the geese, God gave me a peace. A deep peace like I hadn't felt in weeks. I could let go and not be in control. I could be totally insufficient to run my life. And that was OK. It was even good. I just had to trust God and listen to him, and it would all be OK. He was in charge, and I could rest in him.

Even though my life won't be smooth from here on out, God's in control. And I know that at the end of my journey, I will curl up and rest in my Father's lap.

by Hannah Holeman

IN **HIS EYES**

The disease has been a constant struggle for me, my biggest insecurity.

"Man looks at the outward appearance, but the LORD looks at the heart" (1 Samuel 16:7).

Every day there is a constant battle for people to look their best. One person is compared to another by the way they dress or do their makeup or their hair. There is definite competition between people, whether it is spoken or unspoken—it's a feeling you sense, especially when you are a teenage girl among thousands of other teenage girls in high school.

A Disease

I have a skin disease. It is called psoriasis, and it is not a very common disease. It is not contagious, but it is hereditary. Patches of dry skin are on my body in random places, most commonly my elbows, scalp and knees. I have it other places as well, such as on my back, around my ears and on my chest.

Unfortunately, it is not curable. Dermatologists can give me an ointment that helps clear it up for a while, but there is still no cure. I have lived with it for most of my life, inheriting it from my dad. I am the only one of three kids to be "blessed" with the disease. It has been a constant struggle for me, my biggest insecurity.

Not always being able to put my hair up or wear certain cute clothes is something I face a lot. Being in a dress or a swimsuit can be really uncomfortable if I haven't been treating my skin for a while. Treating it is a pain because I can only put the ointment on at night. Going to bed greasy is not always fun, and most of the time I am too tired to put it on. However, it is something I have gotten used to.

My Fear

My biggest fear is that people will notice the psoriasis and ask what it is (especially when it is really broken out, usually in the winter or when I am stressed). Oddly enough, it tends to be the most difficult to tell people that I love or am close to. I think it's because I am afraid that they might not love me as much when they find out about my skin disease.

My mom always assured me that I was special, that God gave me this for a reason. I believe that God does not allow anything to happen to us that we cannot handle.

As I have gotten older and grown stronger in my faith, I have realized it is not outer beauty that is important, but inner beauty. "Your beauty should not come from outward adornment. . . . Instead, it should be that of your inner self, the unfading beauty of a gentle and quiet spirit, which is of great worth in God's sight" (1 Peter 3:3, 4). God cares more about what we look like on the inside than our outer appearance.

As life goes on, I am also aware that many people

have had greater problems than I've experienced. I should be thankful for the life God's given me.

God's Gift

My prayer is that God will use me as a tool to do his will. Maybe living with this skin problem could be a testimony to people who struggle with their insecurities.

You are God's creation. He is the artist, and you are the painting.

Some of you might be reading this and thinking that there is no way that you could ever think of yourself as beautiful. You may think that your insecurity, whether it be your weight, face, body shape, or something else, is not a gift from God. You are wrong—it is. God has made you beautiful in your very own way.

You are God's creation. He is the artist, and you are the painting. Use what God gave you to your best ability. Help other people feel better about themselves . . . maybe you understand what they are going through.

You also might be thinking that no one would ever love you because of the way you look. God will always love you. He sent his Son to die for you, and there is no greater love than the love God provides and is willing to give you every day.

Inner Beauty

I will probably always live with this disease. However, I have learned to use the gift that God's given me to encourage others, and I am thankful for it.

In the end, it doesn't matter what people think. Outer beauty will always fade. The only thing that matters is what God thinks. Your inner beauty is important to him.

In his eyes, I am beautiful. You are too.

A DEAD END

"I'm lost. I wouldn't have even started this whole trip if I would've known this could happen. I can't see my way anymore. What did I do to deserve this? I feel all alone. How will I ever keep going?"

by Nicole Nowlen

I WENT TO COLUMBINE HIGH SCHOOL

I couldn't believe what I was seeing—a boy wearing black and carrying a gun.

You never know what God will use in your life to get your attention. One day in particular for me, God used the simple act of going to school.

April 20, 1999, was just another day—until my world was rocked by two fellow students on a rampage that ended in thirteen dead, including one teacher. I went to Columbine High School in Littleton, Colorado.

In the Library

It was a typical day in April. I was a sophomore at the time, only sixteen, and didn't have very many friends. I had just transferred to Columbine six weeks earlier and hadn't had the chance to know many people yet. I was also the quiet, shy type. Minding my own business on my lunch break, I went to the library to do homework.

I had been there for only a few minutes when I heard someone running down the hall. A teacher then came in to dial 911 and yelled at us to get under the tables.

While the teacher was on the phone, someone pulled the fire alarm. A few moments later, someone walked by a window. I couldn't believe what I was seeing—a boy wearing black and carrying a gun.

Suddenly, it was as if a voice in my head told me, *You are not safe under this table. You need to go hide somewhere else.* But where would I go? A boy was next to me at another table, and I asked him if I could join him. He said yes.

Once I crawled over to him, we pulled the chairs in around us. I was hiding under the table with him when the gunmen walked in. My back was to the door and most of the room. In fear of turning around—in fear of what I might see—I watched the face of the boy under the table with me to determine where the gunmen were walking. All the while I didn't believe it was real. This couldn't be happening. Not here. Not this school.

They walked up to a table next to us and fired. One of the gunman said, "God—do you believe in God??" I never heard anyone answer, and I just hoped the person was OK. (I later found out this girl was alive but had been injured.)

Then the gunmen walked over to where we were hiding and fired under the table. I moved away, but the boy I was with was shot and fell out from under the table. They walked back over and shot him again. I then knew he was dead.

The gunmen then walked back over to me and asked me if I was still breathing. The same voice that had told me to hide somewhere else also told me to lie down and play dead. In doing that, I blacked out.

Out to Safety

When I woke up, I realized I had blood on my hands. It was my own. I pulled on the bottom of my shirt so I could see it. There were bullet holes. I had been shot but felt no pain. I heard some people getting up at a table near me, and I made a daring move to follow them out a back door to safety.

When we got out the back door, there was a cop car in the grass. They took us farther away from the building to a mini hospital area they call triage. There I waited for an ambulance. While I was waiting, a boy I didn't even know sat with me. He was worried about some friends of his, and I felt bad for him. In a way I was helping though. I brought him comfort and assurance that they were probably OK. Ironically, I was the one out of the two of us who was hurt the worst.

> *I realized that I had blood on my hands. I had been shot.*

The ambulance took me to the hospital where I found out exactly what had happened to me. I had taken one gunshot through the stomach from the right side to the left side. Nine pieces of buckshot went through me. (Five are still in me today.) It is a medical miracle that I survived. I spent one day in the hospital and that summer recovering.

That following August I went back to school and eventually graduated in 2001.

One Year Later

Now let me tell you another part of the story you haven't heard on television—the redeeming power of God through such a horrible tragedy.

I was not saved at the time of the shooting. During the weeks and months that followed, I went through depression, anger, guilt and even hatred toward God for putting me through it. But God showed up loud and clear at a one-year memorial service that Darrell Scott, father of Rachel Scott, put on. I remember clearly that day.

I went through depression, anger, guilt and even hatred toward God.

Michael W. Smith showed up to sing the song he wrote about Cassie Bernall entitled "This Is Your Time." I was going to tune Michael out, but a voice in my head, loud and clear (just like that day in the school) told me to listen to the lyrics and what that man had to say. I thought I was losing my mind, but I decided to give the guy a chance.

That song changed my life. I found myself thinking about the boy I had been hiding with under the table. I had found out his name was John Tomlin. John was a Christian and was known by many as a great witnessing example to others. I had felt guilty for John's death. But during the song, I forgave myself for John's death. It was not my fault, and it never was!

A few weeks later I was on the Internet talking to someone one night. She lived in St. Louis, and I lived in Denver. She was a fan of Michael W. Smith, and that was how we met. We talked about salvation, and she helped me realize that God knew I was going to experience the school shooting and live through it. She explained that his Son died on the cross for me and bore the pain I never felt!

God has taken control of my life since then. I moved to Nashville, Tennessee, after graduation, and the girl I met on the Internet is one of my best friends and lives in Nashville too!!

If I can leave you with any parting thought, it is this: Seize every opportunity in life to share the love of Jesus. Do not let an ill word be the last word you say to someone. Take time today to reach out to others—the lonely, the sick, the depressed and people who don't have many friends. You never know—today's opportunities could be your last.

Trust Me

You say "Trust me" in the middle of
  this mess.
As I look for your light, I'm dying in
  this darkness.
You take my hands and lead me through,
and you turn my heart anew.
I crawl into your lap; my weary body
  warms.
I cry in relief as you take me in
  your arms.
You tell me how you love me and how
  you always knew
that I always had the strength to carry
  it through.

Your plans aren't clear; but through
  the year
you've helped me realize that against
  all fear,
with you at my side, when all's said
  and done,
my battle is already won.

by Lynndie Wilhelm (written at age 17)

by Steve Orth

MY FATHER'S FORGIVENESS

He had literally poisoned his brain to the point that it no longer worked.

I lost my father to divorce at the age of six. Over ten years of healing, we gradually rediscovered the special bond that only a father and his son could share. Lots of Cubs games and summers at the Little League diamond slowly repaired a once fractured relationship. Losing him again at the age of sixteen seemed like more than any kid should have to endure, but it happened.

Brain Trauma

I arrived at my dad's apartment on a Saturday afternoon in December. We had scheduled time to decorate his place for the holidays and then hit my favorite restaurant for some greasy cheeseburgers. I blasted through the front door as usual to discover the lights off and nobody home. The phone rang, so I picked up the receiver to hear my mother say, "Go to the hospital. Something happened to your father."

I arrived within minutes and went straight to my dad's room. My once invincible and vibrant dad had been reduced to a confused and sluggish being. He had trouble thinking clearly and his memory faded in and out.

After a series of tests, specialists diagnosed him with Wernicke-Korsakoff Syndrome, a condition resulting from a Vitamin B deficiency to the brain. It can be triggered through a variety of brain traumas, but my family knew that Dad's addiction to alcohol had finally caught up with him. He had literally poisoned his brain to the point that it no longer worked. What had cost him his marriage now threatened his life.

Rage and Searching

There, during my junior year of high school, I lost my dad for the second time. Doctors stabilized his physical condition, but his mental capabilities had been permanently damaged. He couldn't think on his own. Virtually all of his short-term memory was erased. He needed constant assistance in the routine tasks of life. At the age of forty-eight, he had to be admitted to a full-care nursing home where he resides today.

Rage overcame me. Expressing the discouragement I felt extended beyond words. Dad had worked hard for ten years to win me back and then had flushed everything he worked for down the toilet. I finally had the dad every kid wanted, and now he barely even knew who I was. It would take a miracle for me to forgive him.

Like most people who suffer great loss, I began a search. I longed for anything that would fill the void my father left. His addiction showed me the firsthand effects of what negative choices do to a life, so I opted for a positive outlet. I turned to baseball. A batting cage never let me down, and the long hours of practice prevented me from dwelling on my tragedy. I committed myself to becoming the best baseball player I could be.

I longed for anything that would fill the void my father left.

One of my teammates provided tremendous encouragement to me. I appreciated the talks Nick and I shared on road trips. He always had the right words to say.

After practice one day, we went to Nick's house for dinner with his family. His mom cooked some killer lasagna, and I was amazed at how well they all got along. Before I knew it, Nick became my best friend, and his family embraced me as one of their own. They weren't related to me, but they sure felt like family.

The Miracle of Hope

A few months into our friendship, Nick invited me to attend a Youth for Christ meeting at his house. I'd never heard of the group, but I trusted Nick. His basement burst at the seams the night of the meeting. Almost a hundred kids gathered to share in some good laughs and lots of conversation centering on a relationship with God. I knew nothing about Christianity, but the people impressed me with their kindness and desire to stand firm in their faith.

Months passed, and I became a Youth for Christ regular. I longed for the hope I saw in their lives. At the conclusion of one meeting, the leader pulled me aside and asked, "When are you going to start playing on God's team?" His question hit me right between the eyes and consumed my thoughts.

I understood that joining a team required hard work, discipline and ultimately a commitment to something bigger than anything I could do on my own. I'd committed my life to baseball, but this guy was calling for more.

A few days later I met with the Youth for Christ leader again and asked him how I could invite Christ into my life and have Jesus forgive my sins. I'd been hoping for a miracle after the loss of my dad, and then I had received the miracle of hope.

Reconciliation

As part of my heavenly contract, I understood I needed my dad's forgiveness. I traveled to the nursing home and knelt by his bed. Even though he couldn't understand my apology, I felt completely released from all my resentment. From that day forward, I knew I would love my father no matter what condition he was in.

I felt completely released from all my resentment.

I'll never be able to regain a normal relationship with my dad. Some days when I visit, he remembers the fun we shared in the outfield at Wrigley Field. Other times, he barely remembers me. But I am certain that God allowed this tragedy for a reason. In a time of hopelessness, I received hope. I forgave my dad, and my Father has forgiven me.

by Jessica Keller

FOR BEN MARSHALL

"Ben is dying in a hospital, and your answer is that life isn't fair?"

Hunkering down in the driver's seat of my car, I crossed my arms like a two-year-old who's been yelled at.

People complain that life isn't fair, and it's the truth. I don't want to hear about "making lemonade when life gives you lemons." I cannot stand to hear any of those cute sayings that are supposed to make a person feel good. I don't want to feel good.

Life's Not Fair

My mom stepped outside barefoot and quietly walked to my car. She tapped softly on the window with her first two knuckles. Shaking my head, I hugged myself tighter.

"Jess. Jess, roll down the window," she pleaded. "If you want to see Ben, you'd better leave now." She spoke through the glass.

"I can't go." I finally unlocked the door so she could open it and talk to me. "Mom, it's not fair."

"Life isn't fair." My mother said the words I didn't want to hear.

"That's supposed to make me feel better?!" Raising my voice I gripped the steering wheel. "Ben is dying in a hospital, and your answer is that life isn't fair?" Lowering my eyebrows, I turned to her.

"Jessie," she touched my forearm lightly, "no, I don't have an answer. I don't know why he has leukemia, and I don't know why he can't be cured—"

"No." Pushing her hand off my arm, I cut my mother off. "Ben was cured. It's a relapse. He was fine before."

"Do you want me to come with you?" Her voice was gentle.

"No." Shoving the keys in, I started the car. Without saying a word to my mother, I pulled the door closed and backed out of the driveway. The hospital wasn't far from my house, and I drove there practically without watching the road.

What If?

What ifs flooded my mind. What if I never saw him play football again? What if Ben and I never stared at the stars together again? I was seventeen and Ben was eighteen—he was my best friend.

I looked up at the stoplight—green. I had to stop thinking. Thinking would only make me crazy. I had to pretend that everything was OK. I had to get through this visit without crying.

I walked into the hospital and took the elevator to the second floor. The mint carpet was supposed to soothe me—people spend their whole lives researching what colors to put where—but they failed. The carpet didn't make me calm. The closer I came to room 247, the slower I walked.

Leaning against the wall outside of Ben's room, I gripped the wooden railing. It was then that I realized I was not ready to do this; I was not ready to make the journey of two more steps that led inside his room.

I had to pretend that everything was OK. I had to get through this visit without crying.

"You can go on inside, Jessica. Ben's awake right now. He'll be happy to see you." Judy, the nurse on duty, robbed my thoughts. Judy placed her hand on my back and guided me into room 247.

Holding Back Tears

"Jess." Ben's eyes were half open as he whispered my name. I looked at him with little recognition. The Ben that had been the leading running back on his high school football team was now shriveled with sickness. His handsome face sunk in until skin hit bone, and his chestnut eyes were consumed by their sockets.

Ben attempted to sit up, but he lacked the strength. Going to his side, I helped prop him up. My eyes automatically went to the ceiling—I could not cry.

"Jess," Ben spoke. "Jess, sit down here." He patted the side of his bed and continued, "Take my hand." I took his hand in both of mine, and he leaned his head back and closed his eyes.

"How have the nurses been treating you?" I finally spoke.

"I want to talk to you." Ben's eyes were still closed.

"We *are* talking." Squeezing his hand, my voice quavered.

"Promise me you'll live life fully," Ben managed.

"Ben, don't be foolish. You and I have always found

a way to do that. We will always do that." I reached out for his other hand.

"We know each other better than to lie." Ben opened his eyes.

"Ben, I—" my voice trailed off.

"I know." He smiled at me. "No need to say it. I know I'm going to die."

His words struck me. I jumped off his bed and started for the door. How could he say that? If he gave up hope then he *would* die. That word was like a curse—you don't say *die* in a hospital.

I turned toward him, but I stayed in the doorway. "Sorry, Ben. I won't leave. I'm being dumb." Moving to the end of the bed, I spoke, "What if God takes you away?" I looked back at the ceiling; my tears couldn't fall.

"That means my work here is done, and he has more for you." Ben smiled.

"No need to say it. I know I'm going to die."

Judy poked her head into the room. "Jessica, I hate to do this, but visiting hours are over." Nodding to her, I turned back to Ben. I hugged Ben and told him I would visit again the next day.

Unseen Arms

On my way home I stopped at a park. I sat atop the roof of my car and bawled. I cried the tears I could not let Ben see. The stillness of night blanketed me.

Finally I climbed off my car. As I opened the door, the inside light came on, and I saw the Bible that I had carelessly tossed on my backseat after church. Flipping to the index, I looked up the words *cry* and *mourn.* My fingers ran over the pages until I found Matthew 5:4: "Blessed are those who mourn, for they will be comforted."

That night of April 12, Ben Marshall passed from this life into the arms of his Savior. Leukemia did not take Ben's life—it actually gave him the beginning of eternal life. Those who loved him mourn, but we do so knowing we are being comforted by unseen arms.

by Jason Gomez

I JUST COULDN'T SAY NO

She offered me her joint. "One time won't hurt you," she said simply.

I glanced at my watch—6:55 PM. I couldn't believe there were only five minutes left of youth group—ever. It didn't seem possible. For as long as I could remember, I'd been connected to these people. *How can this be the end?* I wondered. It seemed unreal.

My friends were excited about heading off to different colleges, but I didn't share in their excitement. I was staying in my hometown to attend Florida State University. I wasn't moving anywhere—not even out of my parents' house.

As my friends exited the room, I stood there frozen, feeling alone, afraid and abandoned.

Feeling out of Place

That fall, my pastor suggested I attend a Christian fellowship group on campus. I took his advice, but from the beginning I felt out of place. Almost all of them were graduate students. *Where are all the under-grads?* I wondered.

Desperate for Christian fellowship, I continued attending meetings, but I didn't enjoy them. I missed being with people my own age. So after a semester, I quit going.

With no friends, no girlfriend—not even a college roommate—I felt lonely and depressed. So I started building a stronger relationship with two guys, Rick and Brian, whom I'd known since middle school but had never hung out with. One day I was complaining to them about how miserable freshman year was.

"Pot will chase your blues away," Rick promised as he pulled out some marijuana and lit a joint.

My eyes widened. "N-n-no, thanks," I stammered nervously. As the smell of marijuana permeated the room, I grew tense. I considered leaving but didn't want to look like a dork.

"We're hitting a club tonight," Brian said. "Come with us."

If I say no, will they reject me? I wondered.

"You'll have fun," Brian promised.

I was still skeptical, but since I knew I could resist drugs, I figured there was no harm in tagging along.

Stealing enabled me to party more and continue experimenting with new drugs.

For the next month, I went to a bunch of parties. The drill always seemed the same: People offered me drugs. I declined. And then they'd look at me funny. Some even asked why I came if I wasn't getting high. After a while, I started asking myself the same question.

I thought that maybe I should say yes just once. After

all, it seemed safe enough—no one was vomiting, blacking out, or being carried out on a stretcher.

One night I sat down next to a beautiful girl with long, red hair and deep green eyes. She offered me her joint. "One time won't hurt you," she said simply.

I caved. I reached for the joint, placed it between my lips and inhaled.

This isn't right, I thought. *I should stop.* But as I scanned the room, I suddenly had a new perspective. I wasn't the outcast anymore. As I continued inhaling and the drug took effect, my guilt faded. Rick was right; pot was chasing my blues away. For the first time in a long while, I was happy, relaxed and accepted.

Getting Desperate

After that, it became easier to give in to temptation. Within weeks, I was smoking pot daily. Concentrating on school became more and more of a struggle.

My parents soon noticed I was a strung-out, doped-up mess. When they begged me to stop and I refused, they adopted the tough love mentality and kicked me out, hoping I'd seek help. But I didn't want help. I just wanted to get high.

I quickly learned the fine art of mooching and began hopping from place to place, crashing on different friends' floors. Most of those friends were junkies, and they exposed me to more drugs, including acid (LSD), cocaine, crack, crystal meth, heroine and ecstasy. Although I didn't have any living expenses, I was still broke—and desperate for drugs.

One Friday night, I asked a dealer what I could trade for cocaine. "I like your pants," he told me. "Hand 'em over, and I'll set you up."

Without hesitation, I stripped down to my underwear and gave him my pants. Broke, homeless and disheveled, my pride had vanished. So had my morals. Without so much as a glimmer of guilt, I began stealing from the fast-food restaurant where I worked, in order to support my addiction.

Dancing with Death

Stealing enabled me to party more and continue experimenting with new drugs. One night I tried magic mushrooms. Initially, I was impressed by the euphoric effect. But soon my mind went numb, and I began hallucinating. My paranoid eyes darted around the room as I watched my friends with heightened suspicion; I was sure they were trying to kill me.

Dizziness overwhelmed me. I couldn't tell up from down. As sweat rolled down my forehead, I glanced at my chest and saw my heart pounding hard and fast through my shirt. *Am I dying?* I wondered. Petrified and confused, I pleaded with a friend to take me to my parents' house.

When Mom opened the door, her face turned white.

"What's wrong with you?" she gasped.

"I'm dying, Mom! I'm going crazy. I'm dying," I kept repeating as my trembling hands reached out to her. Scared for my life, Mom frantically called 911.

The paramedics and police arrived to a chaotic scene. Mom was hysterical, and my younger brother and sister watched in horror as the police handcuffed me, put me in the ambulance and rushed me to the hospital. There doctors pumped my stomach to empty the drugs from my system.

My near-death experience scared me enough to abandon drugs for a few weeks. But I was miserable and lonely—just like before I started using. So one night when my friend Danielle told me about a party she was going to, I went along. I arrived at the party and immediately felt at home.

"Here—have some ecstasy," Danielle offered. I couldn't resist. Before long, I was flying. *Why did I ever stop?* I wondered. *This is awesome!*

Then a shriek from the bathroom shattered my hypnotic state. I rushed to see what was wrong.

"They won't move!" Danielle cried, referring to two guys lying on the floor motionless, staring into space. I kneeled down and studied their hollow, lifeless eyes—eyes that didn't even blink.

"What are they on?" I asked.

"Ecstasy," a guy said. "They must've gotten a bad batch."

Dizziness overwhelmed me. I couldn't tell up from down. . . . Am I dying?

Shivers shot through my spine. I was also high on ecstasy. *Will I end up in a coma too? Or worse?* I panicked. I knew then that things needed to change.

I left the party and crashed at a junkie's trashed apartment. I sat down in the kitchen, cradled my head in my hands and stared down at the filthy floor. Haunted by the vision of the two guys from the party, I thought, *That could've been me! My life is so messed up!* Wallowing in self-pity, I wondered, *Why has this happened to me?*

Then I realized this hadn't just *happened* to me. I did it to myself. I was at a dead end because I'd cut God out of my life. It was the most profound, yet simple, revelation I'd ever had.

I fell to my knees sobbing, "Please forgive me, Lord! I've been sinning, and I'm so sorry. Help me!" I pleaded. For hours I continued pouring out my heart to him. Then, drawing from his strength, I picked up the phone, called my parents and asked for help.

Heading to Freedom

Mom had a friend who told her about a Bible-based organization called Teen Challenge. Through a year-long program, they help teens deal with life-controlling problems and focus on total rehabilitation—emotional, social, educational and spiritual growth. When Mom told me about it and explained it was in West Virginia, I hesitated.

I'd be cut off from drugs, from my friends, from everything I knew. How would I survive? But despite my fear, I was determined to get straight.

When we arrived at the center, I felt rattled. *What have I done?* Dozens of worries went through my head. But then Jim, the director of the program, put me at ease. "Don't be nervous," he said. "I'm not here to judge or blame you. I'm here to help."

I looked closely at his sincere eyes and felt safe. I knew the road ahead would be hard, but I wouldn't walk it alone.

Living Through Christ

During group sessions, I closely observed the other residents. When I saw the pain, frustration and hurt in their eyes, I knew exactly how they were feeling. Over the next few months, we shared our stories and prayed together, and their support helped me move toward freedom.

One day at group, Jim asked me, "How have you changed since you stopped doing drugs?"

"When I was using, my heart was empty and bitter," I explained. "But now I'm filled with Christ's love."

"What's that like?" Jim asked.

I closed my eyes and thought for a moment. "It's like for fifteen months I stopped breathing," I said. "But when I turned to Jesus, he brought me back to life."

by Julia Marshall

SORROW TO JOY

But that night Josie went to sleep and didn't wake up again.

As a happy, healthy teenager, I thought I was invincible. I was a vivacious fifteen-year-old who loved life and had everything running smoothly. My friends and I were inseparable. I didn't know that my life was about to change.

Hearing Bad News

I was at a conference for the weekend with a group of my friends. We were having a great time together, when one morning my friend Josie woke up with a splitting headache. Her head hurt so terribly that she had to go back to her hotel room and sleep all day. We checked in on her several times and thought that she was just catching a virus, so we didn't worry about her.

But the next morning when her dad tried to wake her, Josie didn't respond. Now very anxious about her health, her parents decided to head back home to take her to the ER.

I got home later that night, tired and exhausted from my busy weekend. I was so sleepy that I went right to bed. At about 11:00 PM I woke to the phone ringing and heard my mom in the kitchen talking in a hushed voice. So I got out of bed. My mom said that Josie's parents had taken her to the hospital, and the doctors had found a brain tumor. They were going to fly her to a larger hospital in the morning.

At that time, I didn't realize the seriousness of what was happening. I thought that she would have surgery and then be fine. But that night Josie went to sleep and didn't wake up again. She was rushed into the ER and then flown to the other hospital, where doctors performed emergency surgery on her twice. She started hemorrhaging after the second surgery. The tumor was malignant and was pressing against her brain, causing her to go brain dead. Her heart had also stopped, and she had to be put on life support.

"Will it always hurt this much? Will I never stop crying?"

When I heard the news, I broke down and sobbed. I didn't think I could take another loss.

Recalling the Pain

Just ten months before, family friends had died. My parents had known Mr. and Mrs. Odom for years, and recently we had gotten to know their six kids: Abel, twins Mary Taylor and Allie, Lacey, Kaitlyn and Kirby. I had formed close friendships with Mary Taylor and Allie and loved to spend time with them.

An accident occurred when they were on the way to the beach. A truck crossed the median and slammed into them head-on. The impact had killed Mr. and Mrs.

Odom and three of their kids instantly. Abel and Kaitlyn survived and Mary Taylor almost made it. She was rushed to a hospital and given emergency care, but later that week she died as well.

I had felt like screaming at someone, "Why, why, why? It isn't fair! They didn't even have a chance!" I remember one night, I asked my mom, sobbing, "Will it always hurt this much? Will I never stop crying?" But the pain did ease. As I look back on my journal entries, I see myself going from grief to peace. God was giving me assurance that he knew best and was teaching me to accept and trust his sovereign will for my life.

I realized that God had been preparing me for an even harder blow. Just five days after the doctors had found Josie's tumor, she died.

You can imagine how hard it was. I had known Josie my whole life. We had grown up together and had gone to the same church. Josie had also been good friends with the Odom girls, and when they had died, we had comforted each other. But now, she wasn't there to comfort me. I cried for weeks. Her funeral was one of the hardest things I've ever gone through.

Finding the Good

Now, looking back on the deaths of Josie and the Odom family, it still hurts, and I cried a lot even while writing this. But I have come to realize the *good* effect that all of this has had on me. The tragedies have taught me to appreciate life and to show more love to those I care about. They've also taught me God's grace and peace. God gave me faith to trust his plan, and through the help of my ministers, I have gained more insight about death and Heaven.

I don't fear death any longer, and I look forward to Heaven because that's where I'll see Josie and the Odoms again. I also appreciate Jesus' sacrifice more, because without him, there would be no hope and no reason to rejoice.

God's ways are truly mysterious, and I wish I could understand them. But for now, I'll trust that he is good as he says. And I'll live knowing that he does indeed have a better plan, even though I can't yet see it.

FUSEBOX | BILLY BUCHANAN

A TOTAL LIFE CHANGE

Many of my childhood memories involve abuse.

I watched from across the room as two of my guitar techs worked diligently to set up for my band's show. I'd noticed for a while that there was something different about the two guys. They seemed happier than most of the people I hung around, more at peace.

I wanted to know why.

When I had a chance, I decided to ask them.

"Why don't you guys party with us?" I asked. "How come you aren't interested in drinking and all the stuff the rest of us are into?"

One of the techs, Chris, looked me square in the eye. "Man, God don't like it."

Within a couple of years, we were the biggest band on the Atlanta scene.

His answer stunned me. I'd expected a lot of things, but not to hear they were Christians. Now that he'd told me, it made sense. His statement reminded me there was a God out there I needed to serve, a God I'd grown up knowing but had quickly forgotten about.

Family Dysfunction

Life wasn't easy growing up. Many of my childhood memories involve abuse. I grew up in a dysfunctional home where music was my only escape.

My parents got married when they were young— my mom at seventeen, right after she graduated high school, and my father was only a year older. At eighteen, my mom gave birth to my brother, and I was born a year after that. By the time my mom was twenty-one, she had three kids.

My dad never really settled into the whole husband/ daddy thing. I don't ever remember a time when he was content being a father or husband. He got into drugs and womanizing and all that stuff. That's how my dad was when I was growing up—it was all I knew.

My mom tolerated it for a while. When I was around ten, she got tired of being beat up all the time. She decided to leave my dad, and my parents got divorced.

Through all of that, my mom took us to church. I knew about the Lord. I knew about Jesus and what he did for me. But I didn't trust God very much, to be honest. The Bible told me that God loved and cared about me. But I questioned, if he did, then why did he allow my family to go through so much?

Rock-and-Roll Dreams

By the time I got out of high school, I was really into music. I had made up my mind to be a rock star. As soon as I graduated, I went to school in Cleveland, but then I dropped out and moved to Atlanta. While I went to school down there, I joined a band called Skindeep.

Within a couple of years, we were the biggest band on the Atlanta scene. We got really popular, really fast. By the time I was nineteen or twenty years old, we were playing for some really big crowds, opening up for acts like Alice in Chains, K.C. & the Sunshine Band and Chaka Khan. I was living out my little rock-and-roll dream.

It's weird because my mom used to call me all the time and say, "Billy, are you going to church?" and I would just blatantly tell her that I wasn't interested. I was real anti-God at that point. I just didn't want anything to do with him.

"God, do something with me."

But the conversation with the guitar tech had reminded me of the God my mother loved. The thoughts nagged at me, but I shoved them to the back of my mind. I was in a successful band. I couldn't let God destroy my dreams.

Empty and Tired

One night after a really big show of two or three thousand people, I came off the stage really empty and really tired of what I was doing. I came home and sat in my living room. I couldn't sleep and just stayed there until 3:00 or 4:00 in the morning, trying to figure out what was wrong with me.

I looked over at my bookshelf and saw the Bible. I knew that the answers were in that book. I opened it up. I can't remember exactly what I read, but I think it was in the book of John. Right then and there by myself, I got on my knees and said, "God, do something with me. I know I'm not being the guy that my mom raised me to be."

With any sin, you're going to reap what you sow.

I woke up the next day and everything was different. God's creation was more alive. I paid attention to the birds and the sky and the trees. It did take a lot of years for God to clean the junk out that I was into of my life. But life hasn't been the same since, that's for sure.

All My Baggage

I stayed in that band for probably another year or two after that experience. But when I started writing Christian songs, the band broke up. The songs started becoming more about my faith, and the guys in the band were like, "We don't want to get into this."

I got out of that band and took a year and a half off to rethink things. In that time, I became involved at a church and joined the worship team. I tried to get my head together and decide what God wanted to do with this talent he'd given me.

God's done a total transformation on me. I had the filthiest mouth of anyone you'd ever meet. I drank. I was with a lot of women. I did all of those things. When I became a Christian, all my friends told me, "Come as you are and God will change you, but don't think you have to change to come to God." I came with all my baggage.

I look back and really wish I hadn't gotten into this or that. I'm married now. I wish I would have waited to have sex. But I didn't. With any sin, you're going to reap what you sow. No matter what you were into before you were a Christian, there are definitely going to be consequences and results from that. But God is good, and his grace is sufficient. I know I don't have to dwell on any of those things anymore.

We All Fall

Looking at the world
with nothing left inside.
Looking into eyes
with nothing left to hide.

Time goes by so slowly,
a clock is all I see.
The world has made me like this.
The world has made me . . .

I'm not who I want to be.
I'm falling apart.
Nothing left for me to feel;
there's nothing in my heart.

I've got nothing to lose
and everything to gain.
Wanting to change myself
and feeling all this pain.

I'm so sick of this masquerade
and of being who I'm not.
The lies and the betrayal,
all the fights that I have fought.

But I've found something wonderful
that fills my heart with hope.
Something that helps me deal with things.
Something that helps me cope.

Everything that's bad
and everything that goes wrong,
Everything that seems unbearable
won't last all that long.

You see, that something that I found
isn't a "thing" at all.
He is someone who catches me
every time I fall.

So when it's your turn
and you fall down,
who's going to be there
to change a smile to a frown?
We all fall down.
Some are down to stay.
It's those who have Jesus
that see another day.
We all fall . . .

by Courtney Cummins (written at age 15)

by Sandi Brown

SURVIVING DEPRESSION

I could not tell anyone the horrifying thoughts going through my mind. . . . I hated being alive.

It slowly crept up on me. The ugly disease called depression was polluting my every thought and action. My whole life began to center around this horrendous sickness.

Hating Myself

I am not sure exactly when it all began, but it was sometime when I was sixteen years old. My self-image slowly began to depend on my popularity—or lack of popularity—at school and at church. I constantly felt sorry for myself, and I would pick out the negative in every situation. Since I am a very shy person, I withdrew even further from my friends. I changed from being a cheerful teenager to a lonely and sad person.

I tried not to let anyone know how I felt about myself. I could not tell anyone the horrifying thoughts going through my mind. I hated the way I looked. I hated the way I acted. I hated my unpopularity. I even hated being a Christian because I knew my thoughts did not match up with my faith. In fact, the truth was that I hated being alive.

Hurting Myself

These awful thoughts quickly became apparent in my actions. I starved my body, convincing myself that I did not deserve the nourishment from food. My entire mindset was devoted to finding ways to hurt myself. I lied about my eating habits. I pounded on my body until I had bruises. I just wanted to end my life. Everyone would regret the way they treated me if I could only commit the most horrible act—suicide.

I constantly thought of ways to do it, but I was too scared to go through with it. Then one day while I was in the bathroom, I found a container of pills. I quickly convinced myself it would be the easiest way to go. I thought about what my funeral would be like. Who would come? Would people miss me?

As I extended my arm to reach the bottle, a spirit of fear like I have never felt before came over my body. I suddenly realized the seriousness of what I was about to do. I immediately began to pray and ask for God's forgiveness.

Loving What God Created

It was purely through daily devotions and prayer that God turned my life around. And this did not happen immediately. It took months of seeking God to learn to depend on him. God taught me how to feel his love. It was only by the grace of God that I made it through this depression.

Through all of this, I knew God was there for me; I'd never acknowledged him before. I'd done so many wrong things that I felt like I didn't deserve God's love. But God is so gracious! He loved me even though I abused my body, his temple, in many ways. I did not deserve God's forgiveness, but he loved me enough to sacrifice his precious life for my sins! I was amazed just thinking about what Jesus did for us on the cross!

I look back now and see that my way of looking at myself was wrong. God made me the way he intended to, and he is going to use me for his purposes. I am beautiful in God's sight, and that is all that matters!

First Corinthians 3:16, 17 says, "Don't you know that you yourselves are God's temple and that God's Spirit lives in you? If anyone destroys God's temple, God will destroy him; for God's temple is sacred, and you are that temple."

God never makes a mistake with what he creates. We are special because we have been made in *his* image!

by April Stier

BIG DREAMS AND HARD LESSONS

It's so unfair! Why do you give people hopes and dreams and then rip them away?

A cold, biting wind whipped my black skirt around my legs and tossed my hair into my face. A heavy silence permeated the air. I watched people of all ages gather around me. Streams of people came from every direction, but we all had the same destination and purpose.

I was only one face among hundreds that came to honor the life of Jacob Charles Cushman on February 1, 2001. But I was one life that would be forever changed by his death.

Scared to Risk

With my arm tightly woven through my best friend's, I watched my brother walk on his crutches behind the rest of the pallbearers. The sight caused my heart to plunge in my chest. This could have been my brother's funeral. Fresh tears gathered in my eyes. I thanked

God again for sparing my brother in this tragic car accident that left two of his close friends dead and another in critical condition, still fighting for his life at the hospital.

Jake had lived his life completely for God, and now he was fully in God's presence.

My eyes searched for Jake's family. People crowded around the tent to shield themselves from the wind, and they blocked my gaze. I looked up at the overcast sky and heard Jake's mom sobbing. All of my struggles surfaced again, and I inwardly cried out to God. *It's so unfair! He was so young and had so much potential. Why do you give people hopes and dreams and then rip them away?*

I was scared. During the past two years, I had been struggling with my own dreams for the future. I had big dreams, and these dreams were precious to me. I didn't want to fail while trying to achieve them, so I had clutched them tightly in my grasp, too afraid to take the risk and attempt to chase them. Only in the past two weeks had I gained enough courage to finally pursue them, but Jake's death proved to me that no dream was ever assured of coming true.

The minister began to say a few words, but they scattered with the wind. I huddled next to my best friend to stay warm as I felt emotional numbness overtake my body. When the service ended, I walked in a daze to the car and mechanically climbed inside. I stared with bleak eyes at the mass of people scattering in dozens of directions. The ride was silent.

I buried my feelings during the potluck at church after the funeral service and felt relieved when we finally left for home. When we arrived home, I didn't know what to do with myself. I was incredibly tired, and all I wanted to do was escape reality. I changed my clothes and fell into bed. Tears kept me company until exhaustion claimed me.

"Why, God?"

I woke up slowly. My body felt drugged, and my mind was cloudy. Memories quickly pounced on me, and grief wasn't far behind. The familiar heaviness settled back in my chest, and I pushed back the covers.

Rubbing a hand over my face, I walked into our living room. Mom sat passively watching TV and informed me that Christopher was at the Cushmans' house. Dad had gone to bed, and she was joining him shortly. It was early, but none of us felt like staying in the world of the awake.

I walked back to my room. I couldn't go to bed; I had just gotten up from a nap. I'd never sleep through the whole night. *I could read.* I pushed that thought aside. I knew my mind wouldn't stay focused. *Listen to music then.* I stuck a CD in my player. Sitting on my bed, I let my mind wade through the events of the day and finally faced everything.

Jake was dead. I'd never see him again, laugh at his jokes again or watch him play his guitar again. At twenty years of age, all of his dreams were wrenched away from him. "Why, God?" I whispered to the ceiling. "Why did you have to take him?"

Jake's Greatest Dream

Words from the funeral rushed back to me: my brother speaking about how Jake centered his life around what God wanted him to do; another girl saying it was Jake's greatest dream to see the face of God; someone mentioning that Jake's goal in life was to change the world's faulty philosophy.

Then it hit me. God was Jake's dream. Jesus was his goal. Jake had lived his life completely for God, and now he was fully in God's presence. Understanding flooded my whole being.

All of my own hopes and dreams for the future raced through my mind, and for the first time in my life, I knew I had to let them go. Fear was causing me to clutch my dreams to my chest, and I knew Jesus was asking me to trust him and surrender my most precious treasure.

A decision faced me, and that day I chose to make God my dream. I laid all of my own hopes and desires at the feet of my creator and said, "Take me, Jesus. All of me."

New Perspective

I had realized in that instant that to be a Christian did not mean merely to pay dues to God through Christian service and then wait for God's approval in return. It didn't mean designing my own career and future and then asking for the Lord's blessing on what I decided.

Following Jesus demanded **everything** *from me—my rights, my dreams, my plans for the future, my very life.*

When Jesus said to take my cross and follow him, he meant it. Following Jesus demanded *everything* from me—my rights, my dreams, my plans for the future, my very life. Only then would I know true happiness and experience the fullness of Jesus.

Jake had understood that. That was his perspective on life, and it took his death to change mine. Jake dreamed of changing the world's philosophy and the way we think. He changed my philosophy on life that day.

I still have my dreams, but now I am not afraid to chase them. Now I am not scared to see them possibly fail because God has become my ultimate dream. And he is one dream that I know will never fail. As long as I am where he wants me to be, doing what he wants me to do, then my dreams will come true.

Life is full of lessons, and some can be very painful. Jake's death was hard, but it wasn't without its blessings. I can look back on his death now with peace—not just because of what it taught me, but because I know that Jake's dreams did come true after all.

by Gracie Hanna

MY STRUGGLE WITH PURITY

I always felt so dirty, like I had just been violated.

I'd never had a real boyfriend. I'd always had a hard time fitting in. I never could get my makeup or hair just right, and I never had the clothes that were in style. I guess you could say that I was a walking fashion disaster!

I had a wonderful church youth group. It was really big, and we did all sorts of cool activities. But something was missing. I never had a real friend there.

We lived really far from church, so most of the teens who were in youth group went to the same school. I was the oddball. And it didn't help that I was shy. I usually just stood there in the hallway and watched everyone go by, laughing and having fun with their friends. I wished someone would like me. I wished I could just fit in with everyone.

My friends from school were not Christians, and that made things even harder. We did some fun stuff together, but for the most part, I didn't spend much time with my school friends. They started to get into the party scene and became involved with alcohol, so I stayed away from a lot of the things they did together. I tried to invite them to church, but they never wanted to go.

Head Over Heels

So as you can imagine, when I finally met a guy in youth group who actually liked me, I was completely thrilled! Mark was everything I was looking for in a boyfriend. I wanted to date someone who was a Christian. But I also wanted to date someone who was popular. Mark fit both of those requirements. Through spending time with him, I was able to get to know more people from the youth group. I soon became part of the very group of people I wanted to be friends with!

Mark and I started to date very quickly, and we grew very close. He soon asked me to be his girlfriend, and I accepted, of course. We shared things about our past and our current struggles, and we talked about what God was doing in our lives. I thought everything was perfect; he seemed like such a wonderful, godly person. I'd finally found a guy who was a strong Christian! I started to dream of marriage someday.

However, as we began to spend more time together, the physical aspect of our relationship increased. When we went out, we'd find quiet, intimate places to go. We said we were going there just to talk; however, after a short time, things would get out of hand. We would start kissing. Then kissing would lead to other things, specifically touching. I thought everything was all right. I mean, he was a Christian, so he should know what he's doing, right?

A Little Uncertain

I have to admit, though, there was always a feeling inside of me that told me something was not right. I always felt so dirty, like I had just been violated. But I would convince myself that it was OK because I *let* him do these things to me. I never tried to stop him. I trusted him. But those awful feelings wouldn't go away.

It almost happened, but in the heat of the moment, I finally said no and left the room.

Then Mark started to get mad at me because I was not touching him back. He said I wasn't showing my love to him. But I just did not feel comfortable doing that kind of stuff! I began to realize that he was the only one who wanted to take the relationship this far. I never touched him in that way and I never wanted to, so why should he be able to do it to me?

As my feelings increased, I continued to let the physical part of our relationship go on. I think I was scared because I finally had someone who loved me. He made me feel so special, and I didn't want to lose that.

It was also so hard for me because everyone else in the youth group thought it was so wonderful that we were dating. They would always tell me how lucky I was to be dating Mark. They didn't know of the struggle that was going on inside me. But it seemed like I was the only one who was uncomfortable with our relationship.

Over the Line

Then one day Mark wanted to take things further. Though in my mind I had justified our other actions, sex was one thing that I knew was definitely wrong for a relationship outside of marriage. I kept telling him no every time he pressured me about it. I did not want to lose my virginity. He kept on pressuring me, though.

Mark would tell me that I really didn't love him because I wouldn't do it. I remember being taught in school and church not to listen to that type of plea because it wasn't sincere. But it was so hard to refuse. I didn't want him to break up with me because then I would lose this love and acceptance I was finally feeling. The temptation was much stronger than I ever thought it would be!

I was so confused. I was getting ready to go off to college in another state in just a few days. I had no idea what to do. I didn't want to lose my boyfriend. But I didn't want to be pressured to have sex. He kept reminding me that we "needed" to do this before I went off to college. But what would happen if I got pregnant? How would I ever finish college if I had a child?

Our last night together before I left for college was full of mixed emotions. I knew I would miss him terribly. I didn't want to leave. But on the other hand, I would be relieved not to be near that sexual pressure anymore.

That last night proved to be the hardest for me. The pressure to give in to sex was stronger than ever, and I let myself get pushed into a situation in which it almost happened. But I know that God was helping me because in the heat of the moment, I finally said no and left the room.

A New Start

I was so surprised at the relief I felt. I thought I'd regret my decision and wish that we had shared one last passionate moment. I thought I'd be scared to possibly lose Mark as my boyfriend. Instead, I was so happy finally to have stood my ground and refused to give in. Although we did many things I regret, I'm thankful I did not lose my virginity.

Now, as I'm starting down the road to my new home at college, I'm so relieved. I'm relieved to be able to start fresh and new. I'm relieved to be away from the constant pressure.

Deep down inside, I know that our long-distance relationship will never last because it was built purely on physical things. I was afraid to admit this before, but I noticed that Mark had already become close friends with another girl while I was still in town. It hurts me to think that I was used just for his physical pleasures. It hurts me to think that he could so quickly replace me. I don't know what his intentions are with this other girl, but my gut feeling is that he is seeking out another physical relationship.

I feel hurt and betrayed by Mark. But he doesn't deserve to be with me if he's not going to treat me with respect. I'm going to wait until God sends along a guy who doesn't constantly push me to become physical. I want to have a boyfriend who respects my standard of purity.

by Thad Fisher

THE SCENT OF GOD

In my father's anger and drunkenness, he had left a mark on me I would never forget.

I lived in a small trailer in Missouri. If you walked into my room, you would see an old broken TV to your right, a small single-size bed in front of you and a tiny closet to your left. The closet held the few strands of cloth I was able to wear during the week; the minuscule closet also was the location of the water lines to the washer. Every so often I would awaken to find that the lines had become disconnected, and there would be only wet clothes to put on.

I was ashamed. I asked God, "Why do I have to live here?"

My Earthly Father

I can remember the night vividly. After returning from a Bible study with the youth group, I went to my room to pray. As I was praying silently, I felt that there was something wrong about my small room. As I looked up, I recognized all the things about my room with only one exception. My father, overshadowing all that was small, had made his way into my room.

By his posture and the glare in his eyes, I could tell that my father had been working on, or even finished, a 12-pack from the local convenience store. (Not a 12-pack of pop. It would be the usual 12-pack of beer, often stocked in our refrigerator. I remember many days that there was more beer in our refrigerator than food.) As he stood there, I wondered what his intentions were.

My father was no stranger to anger and confrontations. Walking slowly to me, he questioned what I had been doing for the evening. Accusation after accusation was thrown my way. He told me that I was being brainwashed by the local church. As spit and profanities flew like bombs from his mouth, I couldn't do anything but wonder why my father, whom God had provided for me, was treating me this way.

Then it happened, like a flash of lightning. With his fist raised, he said, "No way are you going back to church." *Wham*! I could feel myself floating. In my father's anger and drunkenness, he had left a mark on me I would never forget. At first I didn't know what happened. But I was lying on my bed, and I realized: my father had struck me in the temple for worshiping my true Father.

My Church Parents

The senior minister of my church took me under his wing. I don't remember talking to him too much about my family life; I think he just somehow knew that I didn't have it all that good. He made himself available.

At 12:00 o'clock at night some friends and I would go over to his apartment on the south side of town and just knock and go away laughing. Never did he complain about our immature shenanigans. The love of God the Father was shown to me through him. With anything and everything, I could go to him.

The minister and his wife were the ideal parents. I remember the first time I met his wife. I had a cold when I went to church, and she patted me on the back and told me to go to the store to get antihistamine. This small suggestion showed me that she actually had a concern for my well-being.

Through the church, God has shown me what it is to be a part of a true family.

Within the next few months, I was considering them my church parents. At least three times a week I would be sitting with them at their dinner table, sharing how my life was going. They reached out and took me in!

My Heavenly Father

"I will be a Father to you, and you will be my sons and daughters, says the Lord Almighty" (2 Corinthians 6:18). Wow, the God of the universe wants to be my Father. It took me a while to understand this. I do know that, despite everything, my earthly father loves me; however, the God of the universe promises me that, whatever I am going through, he will be the ultimate Father.

Through the church, God has shown me what it is to be a part of a true family, with God leading all of us in our particular roles. Through my church and the family God has provided me with, I can see how much my true heavenly Father loves me.

Now when I'm in my small room, with my small bed and my small closet at Bible college, I put my head down in prayer and sense something in the room. When I look up, I don't see a father who is going to break my spirit; I see a Father who lets his Son shine on my face.

God pulls me close, to his very heart. And as I'm there, I no longer remember the smell of alcohol on my earthly father, but I press my nose to his chest and take in a huge breath of the Father's scent. What I smell is the scent of love.

Emptiness No More

Deep down in the crevices of my soul,
There lies in wait a swirling hole.
I try to fill it again and again.
But this pit remains empty;
    It never ends.

Emptiness is filled with
    agony and depression.
Can't stand this darkness;
I'm weary of this oppression.

I drop to my knees from
    the weight on my back;
I cry out to God, revealing
    all my soul lacks.

I lie there in waiting,
    expecting no reply,
As if it were hopeless, as if I
    were speaking to the sky.

All is quiet. Then I hear
    a still small voice.

Then like rushing waters,
I'm filled with joy and hope.

Lord Jesus Christ has blessed my name;
He made me white and cleaned the stain.
Deep down in the crevice of my soul
Lies no emptiness. Thanks be
to God, Jesus is in control.

by Carl Tsangarides (written at age 18)

by Jeanette Hanscome

THE LORD IS CLOSE TO THE BROKENHEARTED

I had spent the first half of the day in shock.

"The LORD is close to the brokenhearted and saves those who are crushed in spirit" (Psalm 34:18).

Snuggled on the couch with my favorite comforter and pillow, I pulled out Grandma's copy of *Little Women*. I ran my hand over the plain hard cover, then opened it up to the place where she had written her name, Margaret Kronberg. Taking in that wonderful old book smell, I wondered how many times Grandma had curled up at night with this obviously much-read story.

A Precious Gift

Until that night I had felt guilty for having the precious book. I got it when Mom and Dad sold Grandma's house in order to keep her in a good nursing home—

the place she'd lived in since Alzheimer's disease made it impossible for her to live at home.

"If you see anything that you want, take it," Mom had told me, with a hint of melancholy in her voice. "She would rather we enjoy her things than have them sold at a garage sale or given away to strangers who won't appreciate them."

So along with some pretty tea cups and a few other items that Mom knew Grandma would want me to have, I took home a stack of books including *Little Women*. At the time I felt like I'd robbed my grandmother's house.

But tonight, hours after finding out that Grandma had passed away in her sleep, I was grateful to have her books, especially this one.

All Alone

I had spent the first half of the day in shock and the last half calling friends to let them know what had happened. One friend had said she'd call me later, but the phone never rang. Now, with everyone else in my family either gone or asleep, I wished that my friend would call, even if it was late. For the first time all day I felt sad. Why did sadness feel so strange, alone with Grandma's copy of *Little Women*?

"God," I prayed, "why do I have to be alone tonight of all nights?" In some ways, even *he* felt far away.

Of course, in my heart I knew that no matter how I felt, God had not gone anywhere. My friends could leave me alone in a time of need, but I could never really be abandoned, not when I was God's child.

Sharing the Moments

To get my mind off how I felt, I began to turn battered pages and read a couple of chapters from the book in my hands. It was still one of my favorites. It comforted me to enjoy scenes that Grandma must have lost herself in again and again, back in the days before television, CD players and computers. Once more I began to wish that someone could be with me to share this bittersweet moment.

Somebody is, I suddenly realized. "The LORD is close to the brokenhearted."

Fighting back tears, I realized the Lord Jesus wanted to share this moment with me. He wanted to be there as I remembered the hours Grandma spent reading to me, passing down her love of books. Or the many times I ran up to her with some silly kids' book and insisted, "Grandma you have to read this, it's sooooo good," and proudly watched her flip through it. Although still feeling sadness, I found unexplainable joy and peace in letting God be close to me, allowing him to be my friend and comforter as I read Grandma's book and let memories of her race through my head.

"God, why do I have to be alone tonight of all nights?"

I closed my eyes over an hour later, still savoring the last few lines I'd read from *Little Women* and still feeling my Lord's closeness. The next week was going to be hard. Not only did I have a funeral to get through, but also I needed to hold myself together for ordinary daily activities, including a singing rehearsal the very next morning. But if I could just hold onto the peace of this night, I felt sure I could get through the days ahead.

Just When I Needed

When I look back now, I am still touched by how many times and in how many different ways I felt God's closeness during that difficult week.

I felt the Lord standing by my side as I shared some special memories of Grandma at her funeral service and then sang "How Great Thou Art." He kept me strong through music and drama rehearsals for a program that I was doing at a women's ministry brunch at our church, only a few days after Grandma's funeral.

If I could just hold onto the peace of this night, I felt sure I could get through the days ahead.

And to show me that he would never let me grieve alone, God sent a friend to soothe me with a hug, a listening ear and lots of tissues on the Sunday when all the emotions hit me at once and I started crying at church.

Then there were cards that came in the mail just when I needed to know that somebody cared that I was grieving. I heard songs on the radio and read Bible verses during my quiet time that spoke to me with the exact words I needed to cheer me up or make me cry. One afternoon, when I was feeling down, I even had a huge butterfly follow me around our backyard as I watered the rosebushes. It danced around me until my spirits lifted, and then it flew over the fence.

Calling on God

Since that night when I curled up with Grandma's copy of *Little Women*, there have been plenty of other dark days when I've felt alone for different reasons. I still have lonely moments when I decide that I've been abandoned because my friends can't be reached. But I am learning to be a lot quicker about calling on the one who will never abandon me. I flash back to times, such as the week of Grandma's funeral, and recall all the ways that God let me feel his closeness. I pray, "Lord, help me not to forget that you are with me in this."

It is usually then that I begin to hear God speak through his Word or in a line of a Christian song, feel his touch in a hug from a friend or see him smile at me through the beauty of nature. Then that unexplainable peace and joy begin to return, when I can step out of my despair and listen to the Lord whisper: *I'm here, close to the brokenhearted*.

A MAJOR INTERSECTION

"I came to a crossroads of some sort. I could keep going on the passage I came from. Or I could veer off in a new direction. It looks safer to stay on course. The other way seems riskier and different . . . yet intriguing. I close my eyes and take a step. I'm on the new passageway. I'm not sure where I'm going or what might be required of me. But I'll see."

by Melissa Hill

GOD, USE ME

I was overwhelmed at meeting someone so different from me and so sad at how difficult his life was.

I stood holding my tray, scanning the tables for a place to sit. I looked down at my food: a hot dog, baked beans and corn chips. Nothing I wanted to eat. I pulled my eyes back up to see a hundred or so homeless people, mainly men, many of them twice my age.

Why am I here? I took a deep breath and prayed. *God, use me.*

I picked a seat at a table with about six men in shabby, smelling clothes and my friend Jason from the ministry group I was traveling with. Jason and I tried to start a conversation while we all ate.

"So where are you from? Do you have any family?"

What do you talk to homeless people about?

Mostly we got one-word, quick, gruff answers. "Denver." "No."

All of the men ate quickly and left. But one stayed. Jason and I moved into the chairs on either side of him so we could hear his quiet voice as he talked. We asked him questions about his life, his past.

Sompong from Thailand

His name was Sompong. "Call me Som. That's what my friends call me." He was in his thirties. Born in Bangkok, Thailand, he came with his family to the United States while he was still young to escape the turmoil that surrounded the Vietnam War. Eventually they settled somewhere in Alabama, where he'd spent most of his life.

"When did you come here to Atlanta?" I asked.

"Three years ago. My parents die. I live with my brother but he tell me to leave. So I come here to Atlanta. I work in warehouse driving forklift, but they fire me. So I move to the shelter. I try to find a job."

He pulled a folded résumé and cover letter out of his pocket and handed it to me. They were both nicely typed and well written. He'd had help with them. There were four or five past jobs listed.

"No one hire me. Economy bad."

I nodded.

The conversation stalled. I was overwhelmed at meeting someone so different from me and so sad at how difficult his life was.

"Who Was Jesus?"

Som asked us where we were from and why we'd come here. We told him we'd come with a ministry group from our school in Ohio. We wanted to get to know homeless people and give them what help we could and to share our lives with them. Because we were Christians.

He nodded. "The shelter gave me Bible. They preach to us. They pray when we eat." He paused. Then he started to asked questions—basic questions, deep questions. "Who was Jesus? Did he die to save *everybody*? What happens if I mess up?"

We explained things to him as well as we could, trying to clear up the things he didn't understand. We tried to help him understand what it really means to know God.

We talked for about another hour, until he had to leave to get to the shelter before it closed for the night. Before he left, we prayed with him. He thanked us for talking with him and left.

No One but Us

Jason and I sat stunned at how God had used us. Som was so different from us. Almost twice as old. From somewhere so far away. A life so much harder than our blessed middle-class existence. Yet God had chosen to use *us*.

Som had the Bible (if he was even able to read it). He'd been prayed for and preached at. But no one had ever cared about him. No one had ever shared life with him or had ever wanted to know about him, to help him know Christ.

The experience left me awestruck and amazed at how God uses weak, scared, unlikely Christians to draw people closer to him. We just have to be willing to be used by him.

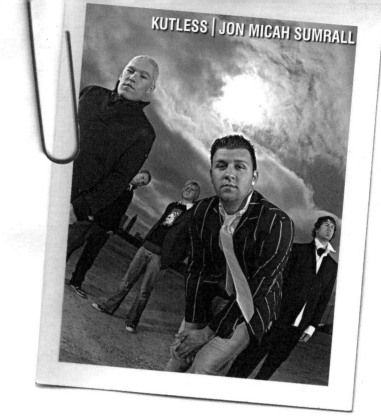

KUTLESS | JON MICAH SUMRALL

STRIVING FOR SERVANTHOOD

After years of working hard, I could finally relax and let others do the work.

I leaned back in my chair and took another chug of my drink as I watched the band who was the opening act of the concert unload their trailer. It was nice after years of opening for other bands to be able to sit back before a concert and let others set up. Finally, we were headlining a tour. We had techs to help us tune our guitars and drums. We had a crew who unloaded our gear. After years of working hard, I could now relax and let others do the work.

A tug pulled at my heart, and guilt flashed through my mind. I quirked an eyebrow. What did I have to feel guilty about? There was nothing wrong with relaxing before a concert. Every band has to pay its dues and work for a while without a crew to help them.

I've got the testimony that you can grow up and stay strong, even as a pastor's kid.

I took another chug of soda and tried to relax. Guilt continued to haunt me, though, as I watched the members of our opening band walk back and forth with their equipment. Thoughts of my parents fluttered through my mind, and I wondered what they would do in this situation. They'd been a great example to me in my faith over the years and stressed the importance of setting a good example for others.

Pastor's Kid

I grew up as a pastor's kid, but unlike what you may think, I wasn't the typical rebellious bad boy. In fact, I loved my time growing up in church.

It was really cool because I grew up in a great church. In a lot of churches, people grow up being told you can't do this or that. I've seen a lot of pastors' kids go off the deep end because they got sick of all the rules and regulations. Not me. My parents were always very careful to explain the whys behind everything. They'd say, "We don't do this because . . ." or "This isn't a good idea because . . ." So growing up I had a really good understanding of why certain things weren't a good idea.

My dad had grown up in a really strict environment. When he walked out of the house, he totally walked away from God. He was like, "If this is what God's like, then I don't want anything to do with him." My dad learned a lot from his past and didn't want me to make the same mistakes. I've got the testimony that you can grow up and stay strong, even as a pastor's kid.

Future Plans

I'd played soccer throughout high school and even made it to college on a soccer scholarship. It was a childhood dream of mine to go pro one day, but not something I seriously pursued. Being in the hospital every year with sports injuries makes you rethink things.

My college teammates had a totally different lifestyle than I did. They tried to get me to join them a lot of times. I'd say, "I'm not into that." It's cool because after a while they were able to respect my faith and me, more so than if I would have given in, I think. It made me a little different, and they knew that I really believed in what I was living. I wasn't wishy-washy.

I really felt God putting it on my heart to do music.

I wondered for a while if I was supposed to follow in my father's footsteps and work at a church. In college I majored in business and figured that would work out for wherever I ended up. If I ended up pastoring, at least I'd have that knowledge since there's an entire business side to running a church.

Called to Music

But while in college I started leading worship with some of my friends at a student-led worship night. After playing together for a while, we realized we had a band and we wanted to do original music. We went from there. We named ourselves Kutless with the idea that when Christ died on the cross for our sins, he bore all the cuts and bruises that we deserved leaving us without those cuts—thus we're cut-less.

I really felt God putting it on my heart to do music. I knew that's what I was being called to do. I told my parents, and at first they thought it was a childhood fantasy—every kid wants to be a rock star.

"No, seriously, I really feel God calling me to do this," I told them.

No one really thought it was going to happen. For some reason, I stayed strong. I didn't know how it was going to happen since I had no connections, but I trusted God that he'd lead me in the right direction.

One day while James, the guitarist for our band, was working at a skate shop in the mall, he ran into a label executive. James told him about a show we had coming up, and the guy was like, "I'm from Tooth and Nail/BEC Records."

I couldn't believe it when James told me the news. I was like, "You've got some timing, God."

We hit it off from there. It was amazing to see the red carpet, so to speak, just roll out for us to walk down. God really opened the doors. The first year we played 220 shows, the second year 250. Our momentum just kept building until finally we were headlining our own tour.

Setting an Example

As I watched the opening band continue to haul out their things, I remembered our beginning days when we were an opening band. There were a lot of hard days and exhausting work. I wasn't above it, I realized. Though it's easy to want to be served, I knew that God had called me to the opposite extreme—to servanthood.

Conviction settled on my heart, and I knew God was speaking to me. As a headliner, I needed to be a leader and set an example. Was I being a servant to the other bands around me? Did I ever help them? I knew the answer was no.

Was I being a servant to the other bands around me?

I stood up and began helping them carry things out from their trailer. As I did so, I was really reminded of how Jesus washed the feet of the disciples and how if he humbled himself, then I could do the same. For him to kneel down and wash dirty feet, how much more should I just be willing to help these guys carry a case or help them load a trailer?

I still find myself slacking off sometimes. It's a constant battle. But serving helps me keep a humble heart and avoid the trap I've seen too many artists fall into—pride. When you're taking the position of servanthood, it's really hard to be proud.

by Elizabeth Martins

AN OPEN MIND

I never knew the imaginations they had that could inspire me to open my mind.

Intelligent, beautiful, entertaining—these words describe my kids, kids who inspire me every time I'm with them. I am a teenager with the job of teaching a Bible study class for seven fifth graders. I teach them every Sunday early in the morning for about an hour. Most of them are wide awake and ready to start the crisp, cold morning with a bright, spaced-out smile of missing teeth.

Loving My Responsibility

Some of my kids are exceptionally hyper and enjoy making random comments. Some enjoy sitting there, quietly trying to hide behind their morning snacks so as not to be called on. Most love to participate and read out loud to express what they have learned. They all have original, strikingly fresh personalities.

I love learning about the kids and how to take responsibility for them. I need to be there for them. I need to be their mom for just one hour. They absorb everything I say or do.

I am a normal, everyday teen who has both impatient moments and unexpected thrills. I never used to like talking to kids because I felt I had nothing intelligent to say. I thought they had brains the size of peanuts. I never knew the imaginations they had that could inspire me to open my mind.

Making a Difference

Something deep down in the soft spot of my heart told me to make a difference in someone's life. Something told me to accept the mistakes I had made in the past and help kids not to make the same ones I had made. That something was God, telling me to make an impact in their lives as well as mine. I never knew that the smiles of these kids would make me feel like everything was going to be OK.

I didn't know how easy it was to read a chapter and explain it to kids. Before I stepped in class on the first day, I knew what was necessary to say and what wasn't; I knew the moment I looked in their eyes. They looked like pleasant, innocent kids, and they were. Every single one of them was following my directions.

I remember telling myself that they could be broken if I were to raise my voice at them. I only punished when I had to. I have learned that, when parents say they hate to punish, they really do mean it. I finally understand why they say that.

Learning by Teaching

Ever since I have been teaching that class, I have learned so much from the kids, one hour at a time. Their minds are as elegant and rich as gold. They have expressed themselves in a way that makes me feel as if the world is an innocent place. My life has been turned into one big miracle. Through their virtue, they have shown me that life can truly be joyful, protected from life's hardships.

I enjoy being around the kids. They deserve to know what is best. So I teach them how to respect themselves and to love who they are. I teach them that no matter what happens, the only one who will always listen to them is God. He is always there for them or anyone.

I have learned so much from the kids, one hour at a time.

I teach them about how to take small steps when they walk toward their goals and eventually how to take larger steps into their dreams. I always remind them to make the right choices and to develop a purpose for themselves.

My life has changed because of these amazing kids. My life is blessed with joy that could snap a million smiles upon any tearful person. I walk in that classroom every time, hoping to learn more about these inspiring kids. I always want to observe the kids' movements and reactions. They make me laugh and remind me that love is all around me.

With each session, I find myself walking out of the classroom with a heart melting from rigid ice to one that is warm and giving. I am proud of my work as their teacher and happy that they respond to my humble advice. I eagerly look forward to teaching the next class; I need the lesson just as much as they do.

This Is Living

I wake up in the morning
And I'm breathing
The sun shines through my window
Now, this is living

I run across a meadow
By the end, I'm heaving
I can't take a step
Now, this is living

I see one in need
I can't stop giving
The feeling I receive
Now, this is living

My day is complete
I now start my journaling
My pen flies over the page
Now, this is living

He breathed his last
He thought he was leaving
Yet he came back
Now, this is living

by Tekoa Miller (written at age 17)

by Josiah Keefer

GOD'S LOVE FOUND IN TRINIDAD

A moment later we were rewarded by the sight of an elderly woman at the top of the rickety stairs.

I stayed toward the back of our group as we approached the house. Well, at least in Trinidad it was considered a house. By American standards it was more of a ramshackle shed perched precariously on what looked like four 8-foot-long railroad ties.

I wasn't sure about this whole door-to-door thing. From the way everyone in the group was trying to make sure they weren't the ones in front, it looked like at least seven other people felt the same way.

A Friendly Stranger

"Hello!" shouted Rick, one of our more outgoing members. "Is anyone home?" A moment later we were rewarded by the sight of an elderly woman at the top of the rickety stairs. She was average Trinidadian height (five-and-a-half feet or so), her simple flower-patterned dress hanging loosely on her bony frame. But even from where we were standing, her wrinkled face seemed pleasant.

"Hi!" Rick said again, waving. "Can we talk to you for a moment?"

"She stayed by him, holding his hand while he died."

"Yes, yes!" the woman said with a smile, obviously excited to have visitors—even if they were a group of sweaty Americans doing their best not to look like tourists. (We were failing miserably, I might add. The cameras hanging all over us were a dead giveaway.) "Please come up!" she continued.

"Thank you!" Rick shouted back, starting up the stairs. After letting a few others go first, just to make sure the steps (which looked worse than the house) were more or less trustworthy, I followed.

After making it to the top alive, I took a curious look around. The single-room "house" was clean, but the pen of ducks and chickens below made for an interesting smell. For furniture, a hammock hung from nails in the ceiling, and a battered dresser stood by the wall. In the center of which was a framed picture of a nice-looking middle-aged American woman.

We made small talk for a few minutes with the woman, whose name turned out to be Lela, mainly laughing with her about our adventures on the beautiful island of Trinidad over the past few days. (The most memorable was when a spider, that I swear was every bit as big as a Volkswagen Beetle®, showed up in the girls' dorm.)

A Story of Compassion

Eventually we worked up the courage to explain that we were there on a mission trip, and we asked her if she knew Jesus.

"Yes, I know Jesus," she answered, her eyes sparkling. "Betty told me about him." Turning around, she picked up the picture from the dresser. Looking at it lovingly, she introduced us to Betty.

Betty had been in Trinidad several years before, volunteering her time and expertise as a New York City nurse to the local hospital. That's where the two met, when Lela's husband was hit by a car while walking home from work.

There were tears in her eyes as Lela told us the story. "The doctors tried very hard, but they couldn't save my husband. Then Betty did everything she could to make him comfortable. She gave him pillows and lots of medicine. Then she sat and talked with him, telling him jokes and talking about life in America. And since I was still at work, not even knowing he was hurt, she stayed by him, holding his hand while he died."

"We became friends after that," Lela said, brightening. "She came here every day she was in Trinidad, just to make sure I was OK. Now we write letters, and she comes to visit me every year."

There had to be tears of joy in Jesus' eyes when he saw that kind of love.

Putting the picture back, she pulled a stack of opened envelopes from the top dresser drawer. Pulling a well-worn piece of paper out of one, she turned back to us. "And see," she said, her eyes sparkling with excitement. "She is going to send me money in her next letter. So I can fly to America and visit her in New York! I have always wanted to go to America."

I had to smile. I wondered how Lela, accustomed to the muggy jungle breeze wafting through the many openings (both built-in and accidental) in her home, was going to like the concrete jungle of New York. Even in its biggest cities, Trinidad has nothing that comes close to rivaling the size of a New York City skyscraper.

A Renewed Mission

We stayed and talked to Lela for as long as we could, chatting about Trinidad and being Christians. But soon it was time for us to leave. After inviting her to the drama and music program our group of fifty teenagers was putting on later that night, we descended the steps and headed back across the village.

Walking along, listening to the others discuss our day, I couldn't help marveling at what a difference one person can make. Lela may never have accepted Christ if it hadn't been for Betty—just one woman who had cared enough to take time away from her family to go to another country and hold a complete stranger's bloody hand as he died. There had to be tears of joy in Jesus' eyes when he saw that kind of love.

Right there in the middle of a dirt road in Trinidad, surrounded by my fellow missionaries, I lifted up a simple prayer. *Lord Jesus, put in my heart the love that Betty has. When people see me, let them be able to see your love in me. In your name, amen.*

Who knows what God can do with a teenage heart full of Jesus' love? I, for one, don't know. But I'd sure like to find out.

by Kristen Willey

SCARS

I had laughed at something I hadn't taken the time to understand.

He walks through the door with blue-black hair, eye shadow, and painted-on eyebrows. Black pants, black boots, earrings, the works. I hide a smile—*man, he looks a bit crazy*.

He turns to look at me.

His left arm is crisscrossed with angry red cuts that run from his wrist up into his T-shirt. His eyes flicker at my fading grin. He turns away, looking just as alone as before. The words on his shirt scream at me, burning into my mind, though I only saw them for a second— "Do me a favor. Ignore me."

Tears of Regret

I cried.

I cried because of my hypocrisy, because I had laughed at something I hadn't taken the time to understand. I cried for him, for whatever it was that made him angry and helpless enough to turn a blade onto his skin.

I cried because there are so many more people like him. And because there are so many more people like me.

Why are people so cruel? Where is the appeal in putting others down until they hide inside themselves and express their pain with violence? Jesus had such beautiful compassion—such love and understanding that he gave so freely to everyone he met.

But where Jesus would have reached out to touch the scars on this guy's arm, I laughed.

In This Together

I pray that we remember how important people are. How important it is that we see each other's pain and help where we can instead of judging. Jesus had compassion on the prostitutes, the thieves, the criminals. The unwashed, the diseased—he touched them. With beautifully soft fingers of love.

Who are we to pick and choose? Who are we to cower under what other people think of us?

Love people. Forget your fears and love your fellow human beings. Put off society's rules and take on God's rules. Don't ignore the pain in someone's eyes—reach out and touch it, hold it. Share it. We're in this together, you know.

Never Give Up

And to you, the guy who I so easily laughed at—I'm sorry. Forgive me. I love you. If I ever see you again, I won't ignore you, no matter what your shirt says. I'll talk to you, touch your heart with mine, and show you that you'll never have to feel alone again if you'll just look up.

Never give up. I am praying for you. So is everyone who reads these words.

And God will touch you if you'll let him. He's not afraid of scars.

ADMISSION

OOC10

*591
51.6

A No Pride Missionary

O God, I cannot bear to see
People that live uncomfortably.
The dirt, disease, and grimy smell
Tell me they don't live as well.
Lord, your blessings are so many,
But there are people who don't see any.
They think that God can't conquer their
fears,
That he won't bother to dry their tears.

How can I go on like this,
Seeing the faces I cannot miss?
My mind ignores the sick, the dying,
The children who sit on the street,
crying.

I cannot hold your word inside,
But my mouth is silent with pride.
Why should I pass them by?
Am I too god to let them die?

You have called me to do your will,
To answer the emptiness you long
to fill.
To foreign lands I will go
To scatter the seeds you've called me
to sow.

by Brenda Bittner (written at age 17)

by Ellen McCaskill

POWER IN WEAKNESS

Speaking of Christ boldly has always been a challenge for me.

I cannot remember a time when I did not believe in Jesus. He has always been a central figure in my personal, family, and social life. However, I never had the experience of leading anyone to Christ. I never had the guts to share my faith or the words to do it. My faith was a part of who I was, but I could not communicate that to others. God, in his own good time, showed me the way.

A Little Nervous

One summer I decided to go on a mission trip to Aldama, Mexico, with my church youth group. I did not feel any special call to go, but I had so much fun going on the trip the year before that I thought I'd go again. During the spring before my trip, my faith was becoming stale. I had little excitement about my faith and read Scripture merely out of habit.

When I learned about the evangelistic approach used on this trip, I got a little nervous. Speaking of Christ boldly has always been a challenge for me. I was happy with the nonthreatening method of evangelism used by the ministry team we went with.

All of the students were taught the line, *Culto a las cinco* or "worship service at 5:00." We split up into small groups and went through the town inviting people, handing out tracts, and smiling nonstop. Each group had an interpreter to offer further explanation.

The Best I Could

At one of the houses where my group stopped, no one went forward with the interpreter, Sherri, so I stepped up. I calmly called out a greeting followed by *culto a las cinco* and then just smiled as Sherri gave the details.

When Sherri finished talking to the woman, she turned to me and asked me to give the woman the message of salvation that Jesus offers by his grace. My brain desisted from all rational thought, and I entreated Sherri to repeat herself. Sherri explained to me that when the woman was asked if she died today, would she go to Heaven, the woman had replied that people had to be perfect to get into Heaven, and she had sinned.

I did not even know where to begin—a very sad thing for the daughter of a minister to say. I then remembered the salvation colors, sometimes worn on bracelets or necklaces. I started with the black of sin. With uncertain words and considerable confusion, I roughly told her the message of Christ's love. I just did the best I could. The woman, extremely old, toothless and barely up to my shoulder, said she wanted Christ as her Savior.

I have never been so humbled. Turning away, my mind was blank, and I was trembling. I did not have a coherent thought for at least five minutes. When I could think, my soul began shouting praises to God. Later I recorded a prayer in my journal, pleading for the ability to savor that moment forever. He has richly honored that prayer in my life.

For His Glory

Second Corinthians 12:9 took on a new meaning for me: "He said to me, 'My grace is sufficient for you, for my power is made perfect in weakness.'" I went away with no doubt that God had done the real work. I had no pride, just extreme joy that he had allowed me to participate in his great plan.

God can use our measly efforts to change lives.

God can use our measly, pitiful little efforts to change lives. He blesses us abundantly in the process as well. That day is marked as the most joyful I have ever known.

God can use every one of us as a part of his plan; he doesn't need us, but he longs to use us. I hope that each one of you will give all that you are to God and let him use your efforts for his glory.

by Cassandra Johnson

FINDING A MISSION

To this day I am amazed at the immense power of saying yes to God.

The darkness moved in among the towering skyscrapers of Toronto, Canada. A man sat before me. His fingernails were as black as coal; his teeth, yellow; his hair, greasy and gray. But those eyes—something in his eyes sparkled with hope.

I clutched the paper bag with shaking hands, unable to move. The sandwich, juice box, apple and chips I had carefully placed over four hours ago waited with anticipation to be eaten.

I knelt down before the haggard, homeless man and gave him my treasure hidden in a paper bag. His hungry stomach cried out in delight. His words of thanks touched me in an irreversible way, and to this day I am amazed at the immense power of saying yes to God.

A Cup of Soup

Later in the mission trip, we served in a soup kitchen. The rays of sunshine floated on the ceiling tiles as homeless men and women streamed through the doors, sitting down quietly, waiting for the food to come.

Our team of high school students raced around the kitchen making last-minute adjustments—adding the last bit of seasoning to the soup, taking the steaming bread out of the oven and getting in positions to serve the food. The time for lunch arrived. One by one, the people in the room filed through the line, graciously waiting for their turn and thanking us after receiving their food.

After almost everyone had finished, one man motioned me over to his table. Holding up his scratched red thermos, he asked, "Would it be possible for me to have even a little bit more for later? I haven't eaten all week."

Stunned by the statement as much as the question, I shakily grabbed the thermos and disappeared into the kitchen. As I was scooping the soup, my mind raced with questions of how it was possible that someone had not eaten in days. I screwed the lid on tightly and scurried back to the man.

His face spoke more than the thank-you that tumbled from his lips. I had given him some extra soup. It cost me nothing, yet to him it made a difference.

A Work of Art

Almost a year later, in the heart of the Appalachian Mountains of West Virginia, I joined another mission team working in a summer school program for poor children. One child in particular caught my attention.

She feverishly worked on the daily craft project, straining her wart-ridden fingers to carefully place colorful feathers, sequins and glue on a plain paper plate. Soon these ordinary, white paper plates would become beautiful masks for the students to wear. The teacher carefully inspected each student's work, looking for detail and originality.

It cost me nothing, yet to him it made a difference.

The competition neared completion, and the teacher sought to determine which student would win the prize. The young girl waited with hope that, for once, hers would be chosen for the prestigious prize.

She lost. Tears streamed down her small, dirty face. Going over to her, putting my arm around her fragile shaking shoulders, I told her the beauty of her mask. The tears and the shaking subsided, and a happy little girl returned once again.

An Opportunity to Serve

Mission trips offer opportunities to explore our world, build real relationships, and serve in diverse settings. More than anything else, they provide chances to say yes to God in concrete ways.

The opportunities to serve are endless. Discover dancing with little children on a playground in rural America. Help paint a house for an elderly woman who cannot climb a ladder. Serve a hearty meal to a hungry, homeless person.

In everything you do, follow Jesus' example of love and, "let your light shine before men, that they may see your good deeds and praise your Father in heaven" (Matthew 5:16).

Impressions

The sincerest feeling I ever had was when you made an impression on me. I don't know where it came from or how it got its start, but I grant you it was certainly a feeling from the heart. It was an unmistakable feeling that will never go away, and yes, I'll think about it each and every day. There are some people who come from above that are filled with God's warm and caring love. People like this are those that describe you, with your own uniqueness, generosity and characteristics too. You made an impression that I'm not soon to forget and will always be remembered since the day that we met.

by Christopher Bratcher (written at age 18)

by Jessica Keller

SOMEONE'S WATCHING

Did working at a summer camp really matter?

It is often said that wisdom comes with age, but last summer I realized that some wisdom can only be seen when looking through a pair of less-aged eyes.

Amy

My troop of campers squirmed in the cool grass under a blanket of night as I tried to finish up devotion time.

"See all those stars?" I asked my cabin of twelve girls. "Well, think of how big they are, but you are more important to God than they are." We scrambled off the ground and to our cabin. I lagged behind as they charged into the darkness in the direction of Tumbleweed, the cabin we would call home for the week.

Looking into the sky, I wondered if my being there was worth it. Did working at a summer camp really matter? Was I a fool to think I would make a difference? Did any of my six- and seven-year-old campers understand the messages I tried to convey?

Suddenly a tiny hand clutching my own brought me out of my thoughts. I looked down to see little Amy's puppy-dog-brown eyes gazing up at me.

"Jessica, I want to be just like you." She grew bashful and cast her eyes to the ground. "I'm going to be a counselor some day and be just like you." I smiled and took her back to Tumbleweed, but I could not get her words out of my mind.

The rest of the summer I thought about little Amy and what she had said. For the first time in my life, I was aware that others were watching and mimicking me.

Debra

"Jessica," a whiny voice tugged at my ears. Hiding a sigh, I forced myself to smile at Debra, a camper of mine who was hard to love. Debra was rarely happy, and she rarely showered. I was at my wit's end trying to convince her to change her outfit or take a brush to the auburn mouse nest atop her head.

Yanking on my shirt she begged, "Can you pleeeeeee-ase take me on a paddleboat ride?"

I thought for a moment, studying the grubby fingers that kept reaching for me. I gritted my teeth—she had been asking all week. "Sure thing!" I said with a smile as she pulled me to a grimy paddleboat that did not appear seaworthy.

As Debra chatted about things she had done, things she wanted to do and life at home, I prayed that God would grant me love—love for a child who seemed unpleasant to me. During the hour spent with Debra, I grew to appreciate her uniqueness and value.

Weeks after camp had ended, I received a letter from Debra's parents saying how different Debra was since camp. They thanked me for spending time with her.

Sierra

Our bodies dripped sweat as the sun poured out its wrath on us. We had been rowing for six hours, but it seemed more like days. Our canoes stretched silently into the horizon like a hushed troop of soldiers heading off to battle.

My back ached. My arms were numb—they rowed without feeling. Bugs swarmed around our heads; it was useless to shoo them away.

"Jessica! Help! We're stuck again!" Sierra called as a clump of cattails swallowed their boat. It was the "again" that got me. Without a word I jumped into the swampy river. Muck consumed me up to the waist as I trudged forward.

For the first time in my life, I was aware that others were watching and mimicking me.

I stifled a scream as a snake swam by me. *It's just a garden snake*, I tried to reassure myself, but my thoughts turned to leeches and anything else that could be hiding in the water.

Upon reaching the canoe, I scolded the girls for the tenth time. It's not that hard to paddle a canoe, and they were making the trip longer and much more work than it needed to be.

"Girls, I know you're tired, but I'm just as tired as you are. Just row in the shape of a J. Don't you remember all the things we learned?" I lectured them as I yanked the vessel back onto the path. Losing my balance, I fell back into the mud and came up completely covered. "I wish I wasn't here," I muttered.

"Jessica?" A voice came from behind me.

"What, Sierra?" I could have kicked myself in the head. Rule number one is never let your campers hear you say something negative.

"I know you're mad because we keep getting stuck, but we're having lots of fun. I think you should stop worrying and just enjoy the trip." Sierra spoke softly but knowledgeably.

The night before, I had taught a lesson on 1 Thessalonians 5:16-18, "Be joyful always; pray continually; give thanks in all circumstances, for this is God's will for you in Christ Jesus." My campers had been listening and were now teaching me.

Sierra spoke those words over a year ago, but I repeat them often. "Just enjoy the trip."

by Sarah M. Will

SHOWERS OF BLESSINGS

I had never understood how blessed I am to enjoy my long, warm baths.

I love to take long, warm baths. I have an enormous collection of bubble baths and scented soaps because soaking in perfumed, sudsy water is one of my favorite things to do. To be honest, I have entirely more bath supplies than anyone could possibly need.

Three-Minute Showers

Two summers ago, I traveled to Caracas, Venezuela, on a mission trip. While I was there, my bathing time was reduced to three minutes in a lukewarm shower. When you have worked all day in the hot sun and are covered in what you hope is only smelly mud, three minutes in a tepid shower will never make you feel clean.

One morning, it was raining. I looked out of the church's window, expecting to see only the rain falling on the large, tropical leaves or making puddles in the copper-colored clay. However, as I looked out the window, I saw something that I will never forget.

In front of one of the many small houses made of concrete blocks and sheet metal, I saw two little girls. They were collecting water in buckets as the older girl washed the younger child's hair. I have always had plenty of warm water to use, so until then I had never understood how blessed I am to enjoy my long, warm baths.

Content with Little

Later that week God led me to help the children who live in that area. My youth minister and I passed out toothbrushes to them as we washed and cut their hair. More than twenty children came. Some of them had scabs on their heads from lice. We only had donated shampoo and cold water from buckets to wash their hair with, and I know that I accidentally dripped soap in some of their eyes, but they were content with what little we could do to help them.

Sometimes I look at all my bath supplies and I think of those little children who were so happy to have me wash their hair. I'm thankful that God has blessed me by letting me take as long as I want in my bathtub and use all the soap that I need.

I hope that I can be as happy as those children were. I hope that I will please God by being content no matter how much I have.

A PLACE TO
REST

"I'm here! Wherever here is. It's not where I started anyway. It feels good to look back and see how far I've come. I thought this might be a destination. But now it looks like there's farther to go. If I'd known the trip would be this long, I might not have started in the first place. But now I want to go on. I need to go on. I'll rest for now and get ready for the next leg of the journey."

DAVID CROWDER

THE **ROAD TO FAITH**

At a fairly young age, I began questioning how to accept Jesus as Lord.

The conversation had jarred me to reality. As I sat in my dorm room at college, I stared at the phone, replaying my mother's words. The moment didn't seem real. I expected at any time to wake up and find this was a nightmare, but it wasn't.

Someone in my family—someone I greatly admired—had done something horrendous. My mother's words continued to echo in my mind as I tried to grasp the reality of what had happened. I just couldn't believe it.

For so long, I'd looked up to this family member—a person who I thought had everything figured out, everything together. As I watched this person crumble, I questioned the similar faith I shared with this person.

A Purple Puppet Named Eugene

My faith had been an easy road for my entire life, not filled with the tribulations many go through. I was born into a Christian family, which helped. My parents had been so devout in their faith that at times I actually wondered if I was born in the church nursery.

"Don't be mad at Eugene. I just wanted Jesus to be my Savior."

At a fairly young age, I began questioning how to accept Jesus as Lord. My parents really wanted me to understand what it meant to accept Christ before making that decision. But one night when I was seven years old, I was in a children's service at church, and a guy did a show for us using a purple puppet named Eugene.

The guy asked Eugene, "Do you want Jesus in your heart?"

"Yes, I do," Eugene said.

Immediately, I was like, "I want Jesus in my heart too!"

When he offered an invitation, I went down front with a bunch of older kids. That's where my journey began. Right there—me and Eugene.

"I Have to Have Jesus"

My excitement turned into nervous flutters when my parents picked me up that evening. Would they scold me for going forward and making a decision? Would they insist I wasn't ready? Would my new friend Eugene have to take the heat for it? Would he ever be able to show his purple face at church again?

I mentally rehearsed what I would I say. Sweat spread across my forehead. Maybe I just wouldn't tell my parents. I played around with the idea. It seemed a safe option. But I knew it wasn't the right thing to do.

Maybe faith wasn't all it was cracked up to be.

I drew in a deep breath and blurted, "I accepted Christ as my Lord and Savior. Eugene told us all about God, and I knew I had to have him in my life too. Don't be mad at Eugene. It's really not his fault. I just wanted Jesus to be my Savior." The words came out a mile a minute.

My parents had no idea Eugene was a purple puppet. Nor did they have any idea what I was so afraid of. They were thrilled with my decision.

My teen years were good. I had a great youth minister. Music was a huge part of our expressions of faith and something that kept me coming back week after week. Nothing happened to pull me away from my faith.

Until now.

Wrestling with Questions

As I sat in my dorm, I couldn't get my mother's announcement out of my mind. If this person of faith could fall, then maybe faith wasn't all it was cracked up to be.

Throughout the next few weeks, God placed people in my life who journeyed through the trial with me. They helped me wrestle with questions and encouraged me not to forsake the God I dearly loved.

Throughout the process, I felt my faith grow. The faith that came on the other side of the phone call was more real—it functioned better than my initial assembling of faith. I realized that on the other side of the ugliness was something more beautiful than I could ever have imagined.

Today as I look back, I never would have dreamed that God would bless my life the way he has. I figured when I got out of college, I would go to work for my father's insurance agency. I didn't think I could make a living for myself in music, especially not music ministry.

When some friends started a church to reach people on the campus of Baylor University, I was thrust into the worship leader position. I was completely clueless at the beginning. The pastor who started the church helped me lead a lot at first because I was just uncomfortable and scared. It was a real gradual progression of more than a couple of years before I was the guy who was out in front.

I didn't think I could make a living for myself in music, especially not music ministry.

From those beginnings of faith with Eugene the purple puppet until today, as I travel across the country as a worship leader, I've learned that sometimes things happen that don't make sense. Life is full of stuff I'd rather it not be full of. Despite these things, God's presence can be found. That's the incredibly inspiring thing—he rescues us in the middle of the turmoil, just like he rescued me when my faith went into a tailspin. He's always there, saving us, loving us and reaching out with love.

ADMISSIO
00C10
*591
51.6

Another Chance, Another Glance

I can't pretend I am okay
When my soul feels so lonely
For something that feels so near
And yet I cannot seem to grasp
I won't pretend to know the answers
When it's hidden from my view
I won't pretend to know the truth
When I've distanced myself from you

When I look out of this crystal pane
And visualize shades of grey
I realize I cannot see without your eyes
I cannot feel without your touch
I cannot live without you here
I cannot go on without you near

I won't play this childish game
I will look beyond this present pain
Find the truth to free the chains
That bind me to an eternal destination

Now I'm looking from a new degree
An angle that will help me see
The victory behind the lies
The birth behind those who die
The hope hidden from sight
A chance to live, a chance to fight
And for the moments I am at a loss
I will remember the nails
I will remember the cross.

by Charity Snavely (written at age 16)

by Norah Hall

COMING FULL CIRCLE

Sometimes I hated my birth parents for making my life so confusing.

Sometimes I wish that my parents had never told me that I was adopted. I know they meant well. If they hadn't told me and I found out, then how could I trust them about anything? Still, knowing made it difficult.

An Act of Love?

It was weird having a set of parents out there that I didn't know. Mom and Dad told me all they knew about my adoption. My birth mother was allergic to feathers, and she and my birth father got married when they found out that they were going to have me. The marriage didn't work, so they got divorced and gave me up for adoption.

Mom and Dad told me my birth parents had done the best thing for me. They said it was an act of love to give me up so that I would have a happy home life. Right! If these people had really loved me, they would have worked hard to keep me. Sometimes I hated my birth parents for making my life so confusing.

Not that I didn't have a good life. My parents and my brother were great. They loved me very much. They thought I was truly their daughter and sister. I had cousins and aunts and uncles and grandparents who treated me just like family. I went to a good school and had lots of friends, many who were also adopted. So what was the problem?

Christmas and Birthdays

I didn't know my problem. It's just that there were times I got so angry about being adopted that I would sort of freak out. Christmas was the worst. Mom loved Christmas. She said it was the most special day of the year because of the gift from God we had received thousands of years ago. She loved to decorate and have gifts for all of us. She also reminded me that they had adopted me just before Christmas and that I was the best Christmas present she and Dad had ever received.

Boy, did that make me angry. I wondered if I had arrived wrapped up in a red bow. So I sulked. I guess I made Christmas difficult. I didn't mean to, but just imagine—handed over to total strangers, wrapped in a red bow. It didn't paint a pretty picture.

My birthdays weren't much better. I could not escape thinking about those people who had abandoned me. *Had they ever held me? Did they care about me? Did they wonder where I was? How could they have given me up?* Somehow all the love that my parents gave me could never keep me from thinking about those questions on my birthday.

My parents thought it was important that I knew I was adopted, and they often reminded me. They didn't realize that every time they said it, it was like sticking a knife in my back. When I was about seven or eight, I finally told them, "I don't want to hear that I was adopted ever again." They did as I asked, but I don't think they understood why I said it. I didn't care—I just didn't want to hear it.

Inherited Abilities

I got curious again when I was about thirteen. Dad went with me to the adoption agency to see if we could get more information. It wasn't much, but I did learn that my birth mother had been a dance student and my birth father, a musician. "That would explain your long slender legs and your musical ability," Mom said. "You certainly didn't get any of that from Dad or me," she laughed.

"I don't want to hear that I was adopted ever again."

The information didn't help much. Sometimes, I think it made me angrier. Mom and Dad loved music and let me take lessons, but they couldn't sing or dance. *If I had lived in a family where people were dancing and singing all the time*, I thought, *then I would be a great musician.*

I tried to forget about being adopted, and sometimes I did. I sang in a band when I was in high school and college, and I don't think I ever thought that my ability to do this was something I had inherited from my birth parents. I just knew it was fun and that I loved to sing.

Searching for Answers

When I finished college, I still wondered about my birth parents. I didn't need another set of parents—I already had parents who loved me. I just had to find my birth parents to answer some questions.

Mom and Dad totally understood. They had not

wanted me to do this earlier because they did not want me to be hurt by a bad experience. They always told me that my birth parents loved me but just could not take care of me. Yet, what if something happened over the years and my birth parents did not want to see me? Now that I was older and could understand that possibility, they encouraged me to search.

I didn't need another set of parents. I just needed some answers.

I wrote to the adoption agency and asked them to locate my records. It only took a few weeks, but they were weeks of terror. *What if I can't find these people? What if I find them and they don't want to see me? What if they are terrible people? Can I ever forgive them?*

The agency pulled up my records and told me that, on my twenty-first birthday, my birth mother had written to give her address and to say that she would like to find me. Not only did she want to see me, but also she remembered my birthday!

Finding Myself

My hands shook as I dialed her telephone number. Quivering, I asked to speak with Cindy and was surprised to hear my own voice come on the other end of the phone. How could we sound so much alike? *She even cries like me*, I thought, as we began the first of many phone conversations.

We met the following weekend, and it was like finding myself for the first time. I learned that Mom and Dad were right—Cindy really did love me. She wondered about me all the time and always worried whether she had made the right decision.

We learned that each of us had struggled as a result

of the decision made at my birth. Yet we both knew that it was the right decision. She had time to grow up before she began a family, and I was adopted into a loving family that helped me become a confident young adult. Our lives are separate, but we will always be friends, and it helps me to know that, even from the very beginning, I was truly loved.

"And now these three remain: faith, hope and love. But the greatest of these is love" (1 Corinthians 13:13).

by Rachel Coffey

THREE BLOCKS TO ASHLEY'S

When Ashley was diagnosed with cancer, I thought my life would surely end with hers.

There were days when all I thought about was what I would say when I got to her house. I couldn't wait to tell her a joke I'd heard or share the update on our favorite soap opera. We never grew tired of one another's company. I guess I'll never really get over it. How can you move past losing the best friend you've ever had?

Third and Highland

There is one day in particular that stands out in my mind. Ashley and I had just met on the corner of Third Street and Highland Avenue. We were planning on walking to youth group at a local church. Ashley had never been, but she was thrilled to be invited. I didn't really see why she was so excited. It was just a youth group meeting. No big deal, really.

Later on, when Ashley was diagnosed with cancer, I

thought my life would surely end with hers. Our days of shopping at the mall and riding our bikes in the park were replaced with endless visits to doctors. Our days at school came to an end when her mother decided it would be best for her to stay at home. We didn't eat out together anymore because she just didn't have the strength to get up and get ready, much less to walk to our favorite Italian restaurant. Every Sunday, however, she got up, got dressed, and we went to youth group together.

A Rose on Her Casket

She died in March the next year. Her funeral was on a dark, rainy day. The weather matched my mood. Through the entire ceremony, I sat and stared at one rose in the arrangement atop her casket. Just like our friendship, it too had wilted and died that day. When it came time for us to go home, I felt compelled to get the rose I had watched so intently. I took it from her casket and placed it inside the pocket on my coat.

How could he have let her die? Didn't he love us at all?

I was so angry with God that day, and for many days to come. How could he have let her die? Didn't he love us at all? I didn't go to youth group anymore. I couldn't bring myself to walk the three blocks to Ashley's house, which was inconveniently located on the way to church. I felt like God had betrayed me and that he didn't deserve to have my forgiveness.

One day, however, I took my coat out to wear to school. The rose from Ashley's funeral fell to the floor of my bedroom. As I looked at that rose, I realized that God had not taken her away from me as punishment or just to be spiteful and harsh. I did not try to understand his will. I only understood that he had blessed me with many years of friendship with Ashley and that she would be saving a place for me on the corner of Third and Highland up in Heaven.

The Right Words

Several years later, I sat on my bed, talking on the phone to the youth leader at the church I had gradually come to attend once more. He had asked me to speak at a special youth group meeting. I agreed, but I had no idea of what to talk about. What was I going to say to inspire them? Yet I knew that God would show me what his will was.

I prayed again and again that God would give me the words.

The Sunday I was scheduled to speak came, and still I had nothing planned to say. I thought about it the whole way there, but nothing came to me. I prayed again and again that God would give me the words.

When I arrived at the church, I was prepared to tell the youth minister that I couldn't speak to the group that night. But as I walked to the front of the room, it was as if I knew suddenly what God wanted me to tell them.

The youth group members arrived in time and took their seats. I cleared my throat and opened my heart to God, prepared to deliver his message. A hush fell over the room as I began:

"There were days that all I thought about was what I would say when I got to her house."

by Jennifer Dunning

WHEN THE
ROOSTER CROWS

I knew from the beginning that this was a relationship I should not have pursued.

Have you felt that feeling in the pit of your stomach? You know the one I'm talking about. That sharp, nauseating feeling that comes the moment you realize you have failed miserably. That moment when your sin is exposed and the guilt of it almost knocks you over. If that feeling were to make an audible sound, it might sound like a rooster crowing. At least it did for Peter.

Vulnerability

Jesus knew Peter would deny him. Peter spoke quickly in defense of himself in Matthew 26:33 when he firmly proclaimed he would never be offended to be known as a follower of Christ. He recognized that others could've fallen victim to such a temptation, but he thought better of himself. Not realizing his own vulnerability was Peter's first mistake.

I did the same. I saw others struggling with a sin I thought I could never fall victim to. Jesus knew I would deny him. And I remember the night the rooster crowed.

Loneliness

Senior year of high school was action packed for me. Juggling an after-school job, homework and responsibilities at home became even more challenging when I decided I wanted to be a part of the spring play. After all, this was my senior year and my last chance to do some of the things I had always wanted to do. College was just around the corner. And so I ran from one activity to the next, making the most of my high school days.

Life had changed dramatically during my four years in school. I once had been surrounded by a large group of loyal friends who were my support and relief from my parents and life at home. However, as I became more interested in what God thought of me, my friends made it apparent what they thought of me.

It was hard to know how to stand up for Christ without alienating my friends. But slowly, my best friends decided they had little in common with me and in turn would have little to do with me. I found myself feeling more alone than ever before and longing to be part of the crowd once again. In the middle of this loneliness, I met Jeremy.

Justification

Jeremy and I met at a restaurant where we both worked. It became easy to spend a lot of time with him both inside and then outside of work. He was a lot of fun, but I knew from the beginning that this was a relationship I should not have pursued.

Being older than I by about four years, Jeremy had been out of school for a while and had some bad habits. I told myself it didn't matter as long as he didn't do those things around me. So I pretended not to know about the drugs and the drinking and the previous relationships. Seeing him sitting next to me at church on Sunday mornings helped me to justify it all in my mind. There would be no justifying what would soon happen.

His bedroom was the last place I should have been, but the first place we headed.

As much as I wish I could forget, I remember that night clearly. We had spent the day together and had ended up at Jeremy's house, which was the usual destination after our dates. His bedroom was the last place I should have been, but the first place we headed. Before I had time to realize what was happening, I was caught up in the moment. No longer did I care about what I claimed to believe, and in a matter of minutes I threw away what I had fought for years to protect.

With shame I walked out of his bedroom with that sharp, sick pain in the pit of my stomach. An overwhelming sting dropped me to my knees and there, with my head in my hands, I began to weep. The rooster was crowing, and it was loud and shrill.

Repentance

The cry of the rooster was a call to repentance—a call we all will hear again and again throughout our lives. Fortunately, God's mercy has no limits. We can answer the call to repent again and again and find forgiveness waiting.

Imagine standing in a room with God standing a few yards behind you. He is holding in his hands all the plans he has for you. What does he want desperately to give you? He holds wonderful blessings and a life of adventure and joy. Answers to the questions you carry in your heart he carries in his hands. How can you see what God has for you if you are not heading in his direction?

Repentance can best be described as turning around and moving in the opposite direction. It is what turns your face to the Lord, where you can see that his mercy is only one of the things he gives freely.

Reinstatement

I find it exciting that God used Peter in amazing ways even after the incident that Peter may have considered his greatest failure. The same mouth that spoke "I don't know the man!" (Matthew 26:72) would later stand before Israel and proclaim Jesus as Lord and Christ.

John 21 shares with us the happy ending to Peter's story. He would again get the chance to look Jesus in the eye and answer this question, "Do you truly love me?" Jesus would ask him three times, and Peter would answer all three times with a resounding, "Yes, Lord, you know that I love you."

We can answer the call to repent again and again and find forgiveness waiting.

Then "feed my sheep," Jesus said. And with those words, Peter's denial of Jesus was forgotten, and he was reinstated as a follower of Christ. His life for his Lord would far outweigh his greatest failure, perhaps up to three times.

I am excited to be a modern-day example of the way God uses sinners to do his ministry. When I speak or write about what God has done in my life, how he's helped me overcome my failure, I am often reminded that his mercy has reinstated me as a follower of Christ.

The next time you feel that feeling in the pit of your stomach, remember that there is abundant life to be found in Jesus, just after the rooster crows!

by Lori Wootten

THE LAST THANKSGIVING

Everyone wants to know what I want to do with my life. I feel so unprepared.

For seventeen years, the only exciting thing about Thanksgiving has been that it signals the beginning of the Christmas season. Every year after the dinner guests leave, my mom persuades my dad to put up the Christmas tree and hang the lights, although he'd much rather wait until December.

Changes

This year Thanksgiving is different for me. I am excited. At first I had trouble decoding my uncharacteristic enthusiasm, but I've had a few days off school to think about it.

A lot of generally routine events feel different for me this year, now that I am a senior in high school. Every time I go to a football game or dress up for a school dance, I come to the realization that it is the last time I will ever do that again. I feel that way about Thanksgiving.

I know this Thanksgiving probably won't be my last. It will, however, be the last one like this—the last one like the past seventeen. It makes me nervous to think about the future. It isn't just these Thanksgivings I'm scared of losing. It's everything—friends, family, my room, home-cooked meals—all of it seems so precious now.

Questions

It isn't only the changes that frighten me. Now there are questions. Everyone wants to know where I'm going to college, what I'm going to major in and what I want to do with my life. Last year the most important thing anyone had to ask me was who I was going to prom with. This year they want to know what I'm doing with my life. I feel so unprepared.

I think we leave God out of our plans for the future too often.

I've spent a lot of nights talking to God about my future. I've prayed countless times that he would just come to me and let me know what it is I am supposed to be doing with my life. He never came to my bedroom for a visit, but the more I prayed about my future, the more God let me know it would be OK. He put my heart at ease, allowing me the comfort of knowing that he has great plans for me.

Dreams

I think we leave God out of our plans for the future too often. We go about our lives, filling our electronic planners with our own hopes, our own dreams, and our own ideas. We think we have our lives planned out perfectly, never talking to God about what he thinks, unless maybe our dreams don't come true and we want to ask him why.

God has such amazing dreams for us—dreams we couldn't even come up with for ourselves. He has such high hopes for us, such amazing ways in which he can use us. If we just asked him every once in a while, I'm sure God would love to tell us what he has planned for our lives!

ADMISSION

00C10

*591
51.6

Whisper in the Wind

My faith just seems so far away,
Though I tried to hold it tight.
Not sure where you are today,
But looking with all my might.

Now I long to see your glory;
I ask to see your face.
I have to hear your story;
I need to feel your grace.

Can I feel the whisper in the
wind again?
Can I see your splendor in the sky?
Let me hear the echo in the canyon;
Let me see your glory fly.

Now the earth is being shaken,
But still you are not there.
I watch the people awaken,
But I'm not sure you really care.
Now the bush is burning,
And I know you're here.

The world keeps on turning;
I know you're drawing near.
And I feel the whisper in the
   wind again;
I see your splendor in the sky.
I hear the echo in the canyon,
And I can see your glory fly.

by Sarah Ooms (written at age 15)

JOHN REUBEN

OUT OF
MY CONTROL

*My hands were cracked and raw
from my obsessive washing, but
I didn't care.*

I scrubbed my hands, desperate to get the filth off of them. Someone had shaken my hand, and there was no telling what kind of germs they'd given me. I had to get them off.

After rubbing my hands together under the scalding

hot water, I dried them, cringing as the towel rubbed against them. When I pulled the cloth away, I saw blood across it. My hands were cracked and raw from my obsessive washing, but I didn't care.

Washing them thirty times a day to get rid of the germs did that, but I didn't have any choice. I didn't want to get any diseases or sicknesses. I had to stay clean. There was a lot in life I couldn't control, but I could control how sanitary I was.

School Dropout

Life wasn't supposed to feel so miserable at sixteen. But since my parents divorced, things had been tough. In fact, I dropped out of school in order to work and help out financially at home. Almost every day, I walked forty-five minutes to and from where I worked busing tables. It wasn't exactly how I envisioned my teen years.

I dropped out of school in order to work and help out financially at home.

Because of everything I'd been through, apathy reigned in my life. I didn't want to have anything because I didn't want to lose it. I didn't want anything good in my life, nor did I want to get my hopes up. I didn't have much as I was growing up, and I didn't see any of that changing in the future.

My obsessive compulsive behavior developed during this time. Fear of disease and germs prevented me from doing things, such as holding down jobs for a long time—no one wants an employee who has to wash his hands every ten minutes.

Psychologists say that people obsess when they feel

like their lives are out of control. The theory made sense to me. You feel like there's so much you can't control, you see things you *can* control and you start obsessing over those things. You start washing your hands too much and getting paranoid about diseases. I felt like my life was completely wild, so I determined to have control over anything I could.

Hip-Hop Music

Pretty much all I had at that point was my hip-hop. I'd developed an interest in the musical style because of the church where I'd grown up. I lived on the church property where they held a program that took in people from all over the country to help them overcome addictions. A lot of people had come from New York, and they introduced me to hip-hop. I immediately fell in love with it.

During those hard days when life bogged me down, I would write lyrics. It was kind of like journaling. I would pour all of my frustrations out. I'd always liked writing and had been writing poetry since I was really young. I loved being able to speak my mind, and hip-hop was a great outlet for that. I definitely needed some kind of outlet in my life.

Despite the fact that I'd grown up in a Christian home and knew there was a God out there, I didn't really have a strong faith. I could look around and see that God existed. I could look at nature and know something bigger than me was out there. I viewed Jesus as a good model, but I didn't have much faith. I didn't believe God could work through me.

When life bogged me down, I would write lyrics.

Gradually, I began crying out to God. I felt a deeper relationship with him forming. The closer I got to God, the more I learned to let go and really focus on him and not focus on trying to solve my problems. I still had to do my part, but I had to realize that things weren't in my hands. It was a freeing revelation.

God's Restoration

As my relationship with God grew, I slowly felt my disorders begin to fade. My musical career began taking off, and life settled into a somewhat normal routine. Then I was asked to travel to India for a week. I prayed about it and then accepted the offer. While I was there, it didn't even register in my mind that I was in one of the most unsanitary countries in the world. I just listened to God's voice and did what I had to do.

It was really funny because I came back with five or six parasites. Everything I was afraid of happening to me happened. But it was OK. When it actually did happen it wasn't even that big of a deal.

As my relationship with God grew, I slowly felt my disorders begin to fade.

I spent so many years stressing and losing energy and wasting time obsessing over things. I would rather have just had it happen. I think we waste so much energy trying to preserve our lives in certain ways, and there comes a point when we really take it out of God's hands and put it in our own.

After concerts I can now shake kids' hands without a second thought. God has brought restoration. It wasn't a quick process, but when you hold out with patience and trust, you can't deny the fact that he's real and he has the power to change lives.

by Cindy L. Ooms

WHERE'S THE GOOD IN THAT?

She fought leukemia for four-and-a-half years, but her fight ended.

You've heard it a million times. "God works for the good of those who love him" (Romans 8:28). But you've seen pain, and you've experienced heartache. Where's the good in that? Everybody tells you that good will come out of it . . . eventually. Right now you just have to believe. Easier said than done.

Last November, I lost my granny. She fought leukemia for four-and-a-half years, but her fight ended. Honestly, it hurt. I wanted Granny to be there when I graduated; I wanted her to be there if I get married. But she won't be. So where's the good in that?

My Loss

To find the good in this, you have to understand Granny. She was an amazing person. She was always looking for ways to let people know they were loved. Granny led Bible studies for younger women and encouraged them in their walks with God. She constantly studied the Bible in incredible depth; she loved reading commentaries!

One of her friends told me how much both of my grandparents ministered to them when my uncle was killed. All of my grandparents' friends came over to support them, but instead, my grandparents encouraged everyone else! Another one of her friends shared how much Granny had encouraged her by taking a flower to her when she was going through a tough time.

And Granny was so proud of her family. She was one of my biggest cheerleaders; everything I did was marvelous to her. She'd tell all her friends about our family's latest accomplishments. In the hospital, with tears in her eyes, Granny told us all how proud she was of each of us. She was such a special person.

Even when she was lying in the hospital with congestive heart failure and leukemia attacking her body, she'd always say, "Can't complain," when you asked how she was. I could think of things to complain about, but she never would.

Granny's faith was amazing. She'd always make plans, "Lord willing." She truly loved her Savior, and that was evident to everyone.

God was so good to give her to me. She was the greatest granny in the world as far as I'm concerned! I'm so thankful for all the memories he's given me of her. And I'm also very grateful for the legacy of her life.

Death Can Be Good?

But that doesn't explain how her dying was good, does it? At the funeral, Pastor Jeff said that God was good in taking her from us. You see, Granny couldn't wait to see her Lord. She always said that when she got to Heaven, nothing else would matter. She wouldn't be a mother, a wife or a grandmother; it would be just her and her Savior, "just Audrey and Jesus."

Even though it hurts to lose her, every time I think about her in Heaven, I get tears in my eyes. I read Isaiah 6 and think about her standing before the throne in Heaven, singing praises to God, day and night. That was what she wanted.

So I'm glad she's home. After I lost her, I realized how much I want to be like her and how one life can make a difference. My cousin mentioned that after Granny got sick, the family started to get together more, and we all grew closer. And when she died, I realized how special my friends were as they rallied around me and loved me.

There were times when I couldn't pray or talk; I could only cry.

But sometimes you can't find the good in a situation, no matter how hard you try. I understand. Better yet, God understands. There were times when I couldn't pray or talk; I could only cry. But he understands that too. I would just picture God holding me in his arms at those moments, and I know he was.

Life hurts sometimes. And while it's always good to look for the bright side of life, it's OK to admit that you can't find it. At those moments, just crawl into God's arms, curl up, and cry. He'll always hold you as long as you need it.

by Tasra M. Dawson

NEW SIGHT

In the middle of my freshman year of high school, my parents filed for divorce.

"She is a good student who tries hard." At least that's what my report cards said. My parents called me "the good one." I got good grades, did my chores, and was never late for curfew. My friends joked about me being "the good Christian" who went to church, sang in the choir and actually enjoyed youth group.

It's all true. But where was God in all that good?

For years I went through the motions of church and religion. I did as I was told, regurgitating Bible verses and lessons without any understanding. My parents claimed to be Christians, so I assumed I was. It was expected, and I went along with it.

Until the divorce experience.

Playing a Part

In the middle of my freshman year of high school, my parents filed for divorce. This event challenged what they had taught me about family and commitment. I began to doubt everything else I had learned from them and began to question the religion that was supposed to give me answers.

The divorce experience I endured was similar to the apostle Paul's life-changing Damascus experience (Acts 9:1-19). He had been content persecuting Christians and defending his religion. He thought he was being good for God.

Until the Damascus experience.

Being struck to the ground and blinded has a way of getting your attention. When God restored Paul's sight three days later, Paul was a changed man.

I had to talk to somebody, and God was the only one left.

When my parents divorced, I was forever changed. Until that time, I hadn't internalized the things I learned at church. I was playing a part and following a script, but the "show" was being canceled. If my parents stopped following religious rules, where did that leave me? I had some decisions to make.

Searching for Help

Where could I turn for help? My parents were preoccupied with their own lives and stopped taking us to church. I was too embarrassed to talk to my Christian friends. I assumed they already knew the answers and would laugh at me for being slow. I couldn't ask my non-Christian friends. They didn't have the answers either. Teachers were too busy. I was alone in the darkness that had enveloped my life.

That darkness drove me to my knees. I poured out to the Lord the anguish and frustration that I had been experiencing. I held nothing back. I didn't know if he was listening or if he even cared, but it didn't matter anymore. I had to talk to somebody, and God was the only one left. Night after night I cried, questioned and vented my pain and anger to someone who could handle it. God was faithful.

Being completely open and honest with God about how I was feeling helped me release the burden I was carrying. Like talking to a good friend or crying on someone's shoulder, I felt better getting it all out in the open. I didn't have to carry the weight of my parents' breakup on my shoulders. The cloud of darkness surrounding my life was gone, and I had a new perspective. I still didn't have all the answers. I definitely didn't know what was going to happen next, but I was finally able to rest. I knew that God was in control, even if I wasn't.

Hearing God's Words

When my heart was free of the anger—when my mind was free of the clutter—when I finally let everything go—*that's* when my eyes were opened. That's when my *relationship* with God really began.

When the darkness cleared, I started to see, hear and experience God anew. There was no audible voice booming from the clouds. Instead he spoke through the words of a good friend saying, "Whenever you need me, I'll be right here." His words in Scripture came back to me as a gentle whisper: "Never will I leave you; never will I forsake you" (Hebrews 13:5). I felt his loving arms embracing me through the arms of my grandfather assuring me, "You are loved." When I let it all go, God became my protector, my friend and my comforter.

I would never choose to repeat the painful divorce experience. However, God used it to draw me close to him. I can't imagine living my entire life without a personal relationship with God. The religion I practiced before the divorce was just me being good to be accepted. Unfortunately, no one can ever be good enough to reach God. We'll always fall short because we can never do enough, be enough or have enough. After I stopped trying so hard to reach God, I found he was waiting to reach down to me.

Changing My Outlook

Of course, that doesn't mean I don't do anything now. In fact, I do many of the same things at church. What changed is my motivation and my attitude. I'm not trying to earn acceptance or escape punishment. I give and serve out of love instead of fear.

I sing in the choir because my praise glorifies God. I go to church because I want to learn about the God who loves and watches over me. I am an example to my friends because I want to be a light in a dark world. The activities may be the same, but now they energize rather than drain me.

After I stopped trying so hard to reach God, I found he was waiting to reach down to me.

It took a major crisis for me to see the difference between religious rules and a relationship. Yet I wouldn't trade it for the world because now I can honestly say that God is my best friend.

by Christy Heitger-Casbon

DIARY OF AN ANOREXIC

I don't know how anyone stands to look at me.

A poor self-image. A low self-esteem. A yearning for a better body. A loss of control. These are things that most anorexics have in common. I know, because all these things once described me.

The following excerpts from my journal cover all phases of the disorder: how I fell prey to it, my conflicted feelings during recovery, and the revelation of how even now—more than a decade later—my experience with anorexia has forever changed me.

My Struggle Begins—Ages 12 and 13

February 15

I'm so gross! I don't know how anyone stands to look at me. All the skinny girls in my classes get the boyfriends, the attention, and what do I get? I get called a pig. Jason is the worst. I know brothers exist to make their sisters' lives miserable, but I think the reason

Jason's comments hurt so much is because I know they're true. I am a pig. I eat way too often and way too much junk food. Mom says 110 pounds is fine for being 5 feet 3 inches tall, but I don't like how flabby I feel. I think I'm going to try to lose a few pounds—just enough so Jason will stop teasing me.

When I get to school, I throw my lunch away. Ha! Who's in charge now?

April 15

I'm not doing too bad—six pounds and counting. Another six or eight and I might look OK. I'd love to lose these thunder thighs. Jason doesn't call me "oinker" anymore, but I think that's only because Mom and Dad told him to stop.

April 24

I've made a pact with myself to cut out all munchies (like potato chips) from now on. And I've decided to cut out all desserts too. That should really make a difference! Guess what I found out? A fast-food cheeseburger can have over 500 calories! And the fat content is super high! I will never eat those again!

May 21

I want to learn the caloric content in everything. I wonder how many calories are in a postage stamp. Do vitamins have calories? I know a stick of gum has 10 calories, but if I were to chew gum instead of eating lunch, I'd come out way ahead.

May 26

I've lost 17 pounds since I started dieting. It's getting harder to do, though, because Mom and Dad are noticing that I poke at my food rather than eat it. Tonight they practically force-fed me. They lectured me on eating a full meal, then made me drink a whole glass of milk—that's 110 calories! I didn't want it! It makes me sick to think they made me do something I didn't want to do.

June 1

I've noticed lately that Mom's been putting extra globs of peanut butter on my celery. I think she's trying to trick me into eating more calories, but I'm the one who's tricking her! When I get to school, I throw my lunch away. Then, while my friends scarf down their fat-filled lunches, I spend thirty minutes walking the halls. So not only do I resist consuming calories, I actually burn some! Ha! Who's in charge now?

June 15

Tomorrow we leave for Michigan for the summer. I'm kind of glad to be getting out of town because the cabin has always been a relaxing place for me, but I worry that Mom and Dad will be studying my every move.

July 1

I haven't weighed myself since I left Indiana because there's no scale here, but I think I've lost weight. I hope so—I'd love to go home at the end of the summer all skinny, pretty and tan. All my friends would be blown away!

July 15

I'm having a hard time getting a tan because I'm always wrapped in a sweatshirt and a blanket. I'm sick of being cold all of the time. It was 88 degrees today, but I couldn't warm up. I'm tired a lot too, and I'm constantly napping, but at least when I'm asleep I'm not thinking about food.

> *Why can't they let me have this one thing? Why do they have to control what I eat?*

August 5

Today Mom asked me if I knew what anorexia nervosa is. She and Dad think I have it. That's crazy. Yes, I eat less now, but so what? Why do they have to criticize me for it? I get good grades. I try to make them happy. Why can't they let me have this one thing? Why do they have to control what I eat?

August 15

Time to go home. I'm worried though. Mom and Dad say they're taking me to see Dr. Kirby when we get home. Why do they have to do that? I'm fine! What are they trying to prove?

August 24

OK—I wouldn't admit this to Mom and Dad, but I'm scared. Today when I stood up in church to sing a hymn, I blacked out. It was freaky! My eyes were open, but all I could see was darkness. I fell back into the pew, and Mom asked what was wrong. When I told her, she spazzed. I've never seen her look so petrified. Jason asked what kind of funky lipstick I had on, but I wasn't wearing any. He said my lips were completely white.

A Slow Recovery—Age 13

August 25

I'm being admitted into an Indianapolis hospital tomorrow. I'll be missing some school, but Dr. Kirby says I have no choice. I weigh 73 pounds.

September 1

I don't like my attending physician, Dr. Richards. He seems like a head case. He says any one of my major organs could give out at any moment—heart, lungs, kidneys. I thought he was exaggerating, but when he threatened to hook me up to an IV if I didn't gain weight, I figured he meant business.

September 8

Pastor Henderson visited me today. He prayed with me and told me the congregation had me in their prayers. I asked him to come again next week, and he said he had already planned to. His visit left me with a feeling of peace. For the first time since I was admitted, I feel like maybe everything will work out.

September 30

It's lonely in the hospital. I've gone through room-mates like people go through chewing gum. They come and go, but I'm stuck here. Dr. Richards says I'm not going anywhere until I've gained seven more pounds. I miss my family, but fortunately either Mom or Dad visits every day. I feel terrible for having put them through this ordeal. Each night I ask God to keep them safe, healthy and happy. I feel better knowing God is watching over them.

October 30

I just got released—just in time for Halloween, not that I'll be trick-or-treating. Wouldn't Dr. Richards love to see me scarf down Halloween candy? Well, that won't be happening anytime soon. Right now, it's all I can do to down a couple pieces of pizza. I weigh 90 pounds and, I admit, I feel stronger and more energetic than I have in months. I'm not light-headed now that I eat six small meals a day. And I no longer have to dress in three layers of clothing to stay warm. I guess my body fat is good for something.

November 7

I ate my first cookie in over six months today. It took me forty-five minutes. Mom's proud of me, and I'm proud of myself. Eating that cookie was hard to do, but I did it. That's an accomplishment.

November 19

Ninety-two pounds—that sounds pretty scary. The scariest will be when I top the big 1-0-0. I'm not gaining as fast now that I'm at home, but that's OK. As long as I gain steadily, Dr. Richards says I don't have to go back to the hospital. Throughout this nightmare, Mom and Dad have been so supportive. I used to feel like everyone was against me, but now I can see that Mom and Dad are on my side. I know they always were, but when I was starving myself, I couldn't see things clearly. Oh—guess what? Jason bought me roses as an I'm-proud-of-you type of thing. It's definitely abnormal for a sixteen-year-old to spend $50 on his sister! But that meant so much to me. Smelling those flowers makes me feel genuinely happy—something I haven't felt in a really long time.

November 26

Jill stopped by today, and she said I looked "awesome." That made me feel good—to know that I could actually gain 20 pounds and still be told I look good.

Now I see that being attractive isn't so much about being a low weight—it's about being a healthy weight. And that's what I really want—to be healthy (and happy!).

Life After Anorexia—Age 23
December 6

Today I stumbled across a horrifying picture taken ten years ago, and a flood of bad memories came rushing back. Mom and Dad feel the same way. Mom still gets teary when my anorexic days are mentioned, and Dad recalls that summer and fall as the "darkest days" of his life. Just last year, Dad shared something with me that made my heart sink. He said the week before I was admitted into the hospital, he found me on the couch in the living room. As he looked at my frail, skeletal body, a chill shot up his spine. He told me I was lying so still and silent, he put his cheek next to my mouth to feel if I was still breathing. He said I looked dead. I'll never forget that.

I've come to realize that, ultimately, it doesn't matter what others think of me.

Today

Although I still have some hang-ups about food and often still wish my thighs were slimmer, I have learned to cope with negative self-talk through prayer. And though I've always wanted so badly to please everyone, I've come to realize that, ultimately, it doesn't matter what others think of me. God loves me no matter how I look. He loves me because he made me, and because he is love. And he shows me his love every day in many ways.

When I gaze into my husband's eyes, glance at my college degree hanging on the wall or hold my baby niece in my arms, I am reminded of all the things I would have missed if I'd allowed anorexia to take my life. I feel blessed to have gotten a second chance at life. Thanks to God's love and my family's undying support, I'm living proof that life after anorexia can be good.

by Jennifer M. Ooms

SHAKEN AND INFLAMED

At those times his love is simply too huge for me to grasp.

Romano Guardini said, "How is it that God permeates the universe, that everything that is comes from his hand, that every thought and emotion we have has significance only in him, yet we are neither shaken nor inflamed by the reality of his presence, but able to live as though he did not exist? How is this truly satanic deceit possible?"

Fading Feelings

Several years ago during Passion week, our minister spoke of the agony of Christ's crucifixion, and something in me broke. Stunned, I realized, *He did this for me!* For the first time, I cried over the pain Jesus suffered on the cross. Many times since then, a sermon, book or Passion play has shaken me again. I would realize once again that Jesus suffered to pay the price for me. At those times his love is simply too huge for me to grasp. I know that I am forever indebted to him.

There are times when I am also inflamed by Jesus. At a youth conference with thousands of people passionately worshiping God, I witness lives being turned around and hear messages that resonate with my spirit. I resolve to live so radically for him that it will be evident to all. I aspire to keep my focus on God. I'm on fire!

Hours each day go by when God doesn't even enter my mind.

Then as the week progresses, my feelings fade, and I find that Romano Guardini's thoughts above were right. I am neither shaken nor inflamed by God's presence but able to live as though he did not even exist. How can this be?! He paid *so much* for me—he gave everything, even his own life, for my freedom. But frankly, hours each day go by when God doesn't even enter my mind.

Prayer

Prayer is the key to a life impassioned and inflamed by the presence of God. Prayer is spending time in his all-consuming presence. It is understanding who God is and what he's done for us. It is realizing the debt we owe. It is allowing him to shake us and change us. It is asking for his guidance and then obeying him. It is bringing the things of this world before the one who is more than able to handle them. Prayer is able to make a life wholly God's. Prayer is capable of changing the world.

Do we really believe that? Do we really believe that prayer makes that kind of difference? If we do, we don't live like it.

I make it a priority to pray at least a couple of times a day. But there are times when I pray out of habit or because I feel like I should. Sometimes I rush through my prayer times or say words from my head and not my heart. At times my mind wanders, I get distracted or I think more about what others think than what God thinks. And there are times I forget to pray.

I know that the very best times of my life have been times I've spent with God—when I've really allowed God to reach me in such a real way that I'm shaken down to the very center of who I am, when my heart is open to Him and I am listening, worshiping, and obeying. Those are the most wonderful times of my life.

The Experiment

Frank Laubach wrote, "Can we have that contact with God all the time? All the time awake, fall asleep in His arms, and awaken in His presence? Can we attain that? Can we do His will all the time? Can we think His thoughts all the time? . . . Can I bring the Lord back in my mind-flow every few seconds so that God shall always be in my mind? I choose to make the rest of my life an experiment in answering this question" (*Practicing His Presence*, Seed Sowers Publishers).

Do we really believe that prayer makes that kind of difference?

Laubach struck something in my soul as he related how he tried to remember God continually, whatever he was doing. He shared how this "experiment" changed his mindset, his attitude, his work and his relationship with God. Later in the book he wrote, "It is my business to look into the very face of God until I ache with bliss. Now I like the Lord's presence so much that when for a half hour or so he slips out of mind . . . I feel as though I had deserted him, and as though I had lost something very precious in my life."

Do you feel that way when God slips from your mind for half an hour? Yikes! Until I read this, I wasn't even aware of how often I *forgot* about God. But when I determined to try to bring him back into my thoughts every few seconds, I quickly saw how far from that I was.

We get distracted so easily. (When Dwight L. Moody was asked if he was filled with the Holy Spirit, he replied, "Yes. But I leak.") But that constant communion with God is exactly what I want. It's exactly what Paul meant when he told us to "pray continually" (1 Thessalonians 5:17). It's what Jesus meant when He said, "I am the vine; you are the branches. If a man *remains* in me and I in him, he will bear much fruit; apart from me you can do nothing" (John 15:5).

The Challenge

There is nothing more rewarding, more wonderful, more exhilarating than sharing every moment with God. I realize this may sound absurd, impossible or just plain weird to some of you. It is a difficult habit to start. It requires a singleness of mind.

Constant communion with God is exactly what I want.

David wrote, "One thing I ask of the LORD, this is what I seek: that I may dwell in the house of the LORD all the days of my life, to gaze upon the beauty of the LORD and to seek him in his temple" (Psalm 27:4). Christ must become our "one thing"; otherwise, anything we put ahead of him will push him out of our minds.

But for those whose hearts desire to know and honor God more, I urge you to take your prayer life to the next level. Pray before you get out of bed, in between activities, while you're waiting for someone, when you get angry, when you're thankful, when you have a big (or little) decision to make and before you go to bed. Work at it until you find yourself praying almost continually—and then keep working!

Do you believe in the power of prayer? Do you believe God wants to spend time with you? Then take this challenge with me and watch him change your life from the inside out!

ADMISSIO

OOC1

*591

51.6

I Stand upon a Mountaintop

I stand upon a mountaintop
I scream across the plains
I shout the mighty music
I move the sugar cane

I move the village people
I move the crowds around
I speak of the mighty music
the music that covers the ground

It covers like the air we breathe
essential for life
but not easy to see
so who will it be
who just might see
the air we breathe?

My voice consumes the air
but the air consumes me
without air my voice is silent
oh, where would I be?

I would be lost
wandering among the crowd
but I am not
I am beside a cloud

I stand upon a mountaintop
I sing a joyous song
I yell good news to all
but who will hear their call?

I speak the name of every man
their name is in the song
but who will hear
and who will see
a tiny man upon a tree?

A tree on a mountain
a man upon the tree
oh, is it really me?
I wish that it could be

For I once heard a song
from a man upon a tree
he called my name
and he asked me
to be with him

And now I stand upon a mountaintop
and sing a joyous song
a song given unto me
who else's will it be?

May it come to all
may the music fill their hearts
may they rise upon the mountains
and sing their joy-filled parts

May a world of harmony
sing far across the land
one song
as one voice
the joy we have at hand

May we be taken even higher
much farther than the clouds
to the writer of the music
the master of the sounds

For he is our joy
the air we breathe
he writes the songs
that we now bring

For they tell of his awesome power
the strength of his mighty hand
they tell of his infinite grace
and a new and faraway land

A land for ourselves
the singers of the song
the blessed children of his
not worthy to belong

But for now
I stand upon a mountaintop
I sing a joyous song
if I could be content
then the master I would please

So join me on a mountaintop
and sing this joyous song
sing far across the land
that others may belong

by Tyler Winn (written at age 16)

FINAL THOUGHTS

So you've read this book and the many stories about people's encounters with God. Now what? How does that make a difference in your life? Well, that's up to you.

Can you relate to any of the stories you read? Have you dealt with similar situations? If so, can you be encouraged to continue down your own journey with God and take a new step on the passage he's laid out for you? Go deeper by checking out the index and reading some Scriptures that apply to what you are dealing with.

Never forget that God is right there beside you no matter what you're going through. It may not feel like it—but he is. As these stories show, no one is perfect. Everyone doubts at some point. Everyone has heartaches and pain. Know that other people have gone before you on this journey and have made it through to the other side. Just keep going—you'll make it too!

But also know that everyone has triumphs as well. Perhaps today will be your day. Enjoy the peace God brings during your times of rest and the joy he places in your heart.

If any of these stories have made you think a little differently about God, please share that with someone else. Remember—you're not on this journey alone.

Connect with other people on your good days and your bad. You'll be helping each other more than you realize.

Where are you on your journey? Where are you with God? Perhaps you're just starting out, new in your faith. Perhaps you're finding out more about who you are as a child of God. Maybe you're at the lowest point imaginable and you feel totally alone. Maybe you are reaching out and serving others. Or you might be at an amazing place where you've grown with God so much that you're constantly aware of his work in your life. No matter which describes you, the challenge is to keep taking that next step on your own sacred journey with God.

DAVID CROWDER BAND

David Crowder—vocals, guitar
Jason Solley—guitar, vocals
Jack Parker—guitar
Jeremy Bush—drums
Mike Dodson—bass
Mike Hogan—electric violin, turntables
www.davidcrowderband.com

STARTING A CHURCH:

In 1996, David helped start University Baptist Church in Waco, Texas, to reach out to college students. David's idea for starting the church happened when he discovered a statistic stating that over half of the 14,000 students that attended his college, Baylor University, were not attending church. He wanted to create a congregation that would challenge students to take an active part. Trying to connect students to God's heart and passion, David began writing worship songs for the church and eventually formed a band. Although his audience is now nationwide, he still keeps University Baptist Church in mind as he writes new worship songs.

FUN FACT:

David purchased a barn and a house that had belonged to the deceased Wade Morrison, creator of the soft drink Dr. Pepper. In the barn, David built his recording studio.

Get more info on David on page 202.

FUSEBOX

Billy Buchanan—vocals, bass
Guy Roberts—drums
Ben Rodriguez—guitar
Justin Mackey—guitar
www.fuseboxmusic.com

HOW THEY GOT STARTED:

After a rocky upbringing and some rough detours, Billy landed in a Christian group called Beehive, which was scouted out by ForeFront Records. Though they never inked a deal, those connections eventually led to Billy touring as part of Rebecca St. James' backing band, who christened themselves Fusebox in 2000 to open the "Reborn," "Worship God" and "Worship God Encore" tours. Aside from having Rebecca's dedicated fan base back them from the beginning, Fusebox quickly amassed a following of their own by touring over 25 countries, releasing the record *Lost In Worship*.

BILLY'S TESTIMONY:

Touring with Rebecca led Billy to become more open about his troubled past, which in turn drove him to greater depth as a songwriter. By the time the guys made it through half of the *Lost In Worship* tour, Billy's incorporation of that message within the music resonated instantly with fans.

"The Lord rescued me from a difficult past and I owe my life to him," concludes Billy. "Although it would have been nice to have a real relationship with my earthly father, my heavenly father is all that I need. God is everything a father should be. He's always there. He loves to hear me talk. In a loving way, he disciplines me when I'm wrong. He encourages me when I'm a failure . . . he is worthy of my continual worship and praise, and I am honored to lead his people in worship through music."

Read Billy's testimony on page 131.

JOHN REUBEN

www.johnreuben.com

PERSONAL HISTORY:

John grew up with his family on the property of
Outreach for Youth, a program founded by a former
Brooklyn gang member. Influenced by the inner-city
kids around them, John began visiting downtown hip-
hop shops and honing his lyrical skills in open mic rap
battles. At age 16, he took out a loan for what should
have been a car but wound up being recording equipment and samplers. He soon dropped out of high
school and devoted himself entirely to recording and
working jobs to pay off the loan.

"If somebody said that they wanted to do what I do, I'd tell them it's not a very bright idea and that they need to be realistic. Of course, it was totally unrealistic myself, but it was in God's plan, and thankfully it worked out."

John strives to challenge hip-hop fans to push forward, take control and believe.

HIS CREATIVE SIDE:

John relishes the self-expression that rap music empowers, and as an artist, he diligently strives to make his music personal yet universally relevant.

John wanted to continue that creativity by producing his albums *Professional Rapper* and *The Boy vs. The Cynic*. He saw it as the only way to capture his true artistic goals. He converted his basement into a recording studio and stretched his many ideas to their fullest extent, which is something that studio time restraints prevented in the past. Which producer reigns in hand, John tackled the albums with newfound excitement.

Take a closer look at John on page 226.

KUTLESS

Jon Micah Sumrall—vocals
James Mead—guitar
Ryan Shrout—guitar
Kyle Zeigler—bass
Kyle Mitchell—drums
www.kutless.com

PERSONAL GOALS:

The goals and methods of Kutless have remained consistent: Focus. Passion. Strong work ethic. Character. The desire to be better, write better, play better. As Jon Micah puts it, "We feel so blessed to be where we are, and we want to have a bigger and bigger impact. I guess it just feels like we were born to do this.

"We want to blow people away," Jon Micah continued. "At the same time, it's just as important to partner with the local church and youth pastors. We make sure that the people that come to see a Kutless show know that Jesus loves them, cares for them, and desires to spend time with them. As a band, we have been so fortunate to have this platform to play our music. We are humbled to be able to communicate Christ's love for people night after night."

HOW THEY BECAME A BAND:

"We started in college as worship band. That's what originally brought us together," remembers Jon Micah. "On Thursday night we would lead an upbeat alternative style of worship. That's where we first started playing together. It wasn't until later that we decided to do original music and play shows. Our roots are in worship but even so, we see all the music we write and perform as act of worship; anything that glorifies God is worship."

Hear more from Jon Micah on page 169.

KUTLESS • 263

OUT OF EDEN

Lisa Kimmey—oldest sister
Andrea Kimmey-Baca—middle sister
Danielle Kimmey—youngest sister
www.outofedenonline.com

THE PROCESS OF WORKING

"I think the growth has to happen before you work on a project, and the project reflects that," said Lisa. "If you're not spending time with God and growing in him before you get in the studio, it's impossible to manufacture it. As far as musical growth, we constantly try to expose ourselves to all kinds and are always open to hearing something new. I think that keeps us growing."

EVENT MINISTRY:

Out of Eden's passion for girls had them teaming up with their label, Gotee Records, and Interl'inc to produce "This Is Your Life" Girls Event. It's a six-session video and music-based curriculum series that deals with dating, modesty, acceptance, abuse, parents, and purpose.

PLACES WHERE THEIR MUSIC HAS BEEN HEARD:

Their songs have been on Eddie Murphy's movie *Dr. Doolittle*, Christina Aguilera's *Diary*, *Dawson's Creek*, and *The Chris Rock Show*. They also got to appear on the primetime UPN show *Moesha*, starring Brandy.

Check out more from Andrea on page 43.

RELIENT K

Matthew Thiessen—vocals, guitar, piano
Matthew Hoopes—guitar, vocals
Dave Douglas—drums, vocals
John Warne—bass, vocals
Jonathan Schneck—guitar, bells, banjo, vocals
www.relientk.com

HOW THE BAND HAS GROWN:

"There's been a natural progression from the first onto the second, third and now the fourth record," notes Dave. "The change has come incrementally with each disc. I don't feel like we're taking a drastic number of turns, but the direction keeps shifting for the better."

"It's my personality to be cheesy and tell dumb jokes," admitted Matt Thiessen. "For the last four of five years, I've taken all the puns I think of on a daily basis and plant them in a song. Besides that tone, this record [MMHMM] also has personal ties. There's a lot about making mistakes, failing, how amazing grace is and picking yourself back up."

FAR AWAY FROM CHEESY:

Matt Thiessen shared, "We've also found it to be the hardest thing in the world to say 'Jesus' in a song and not be cheesy, so we definitely have our own way of singing about spirituality. But in the end that's who we are and what we believe in. We hope between that and the music, it connects with someone out there."

Understand more about Matt Hoopes's faith on page 25.

SUPERCHIC[K]

Tricia Brock—vocals
Melissa Brock—vocals, guitar
Matt Dally—vocals, bass
Dave Ghazarian—guitar
Brandon Estelle—drums
Max Hsu—keyboards, DJ, producer
www.superchickonline.com

FROM THEIR ALBUMS:

Superchic[k] has addressed self-esteem issues; they've written songs based on the stories they heard from their fans; and they've poured their own lives into their lyrics. When almost every band member experienced a breakup of a serious relationship all within the same year, the group members wrote about their pain on the album *Beauty From Pain*.

"We all go through these hard times, but in reality, there is a beauty in that pain because it makes us stronger people and prompts us to lean on God in a way that we never have before," said Melissa. "When a relationship is over, as much as it hurts and as hard as it can be, God is the one who is still there."

"If you are down, this album lets you know that you're not alone," said Tricia.

"When you are in that dark place, hope can be an elusive thing to find," said Max. "Some days you just have to grind out the pity party. For us, we've found redemption from these times. *Beauty From Pain* represents the hope that has emerged, and we've come out wise, stronger and smarter."

SUPERCHIC[K] IN THE MEDIA:

Since Superchic[k]'s silver screen debut on *Legally Blonde* with the song, "One Girl Revolution," the band has had their songs on more than 60 different film and television shows. Their music can be heard on films such as *The Glass House*, *Confessions of a Teenage Drama Queen*, *Catch That Kid*, *Legally Blonde 2* and the upcoming film *Stewart Little 3*. They have also held many spots on television shows like *Alias*, *Who Wants to be a Millionaire*, *The Practice*, *Nightline*, *Joan of Arcadia* and countless MTV programs. They've also been featured in *The New York Times* as well as *Seventeen*, *Marie Claire*, *Bop*, and *ReMix* magazines.

Find out Melissa's story of self-image on page 83.

TOPICAL INDEX

Interested in a certain topic? Check out the following list and find the stories that relate to you. Also, read the Scriptures shown below and discover what God's Word has to say about each topic.

DEATH 106, 116, 127, 143, 159, 213, 230

Concerned about death? These passages will give you hope: 1 Corinthians 15:50-57; Revelation 7:9, 10; Revelation 21:1-4

How Jesus takes away the fear of death by conquering it: Matthew 28:1-10; Mark 16:1-7; Luke 24:1-12; John 20:1-9; Romans 6:5-10

DEPRESSION 50, 140

Read how these two men dealt with depression—they were brutally honest with God, even wishing to die. And then read how God responds: *Elijah*—1 Kings 19:1-18; *Job*—the book of Job chapters 1-42

Wondering what the point is? Find true meaning: Ecclesiastes 1–12

DISEASE 60, 69, 78, 100, 116

Read about the healing Jesus gave to people with all types of diseases: Matthew 8:1-4, 14-17; Luke 8:42-48

But even if physical healing does not happen, take heart—Jesus is more concerned about spiritual healing, and he sent his Spirit to stay with you and comfort you in times of suffering: John 14

DIVORCE 94, 233

Some places where divorce is mentioned in the Bible: Malachi 2:13-16; Matthew 5:31, 32; Matthew 19:3-9

DREAMS FOR YOUR FUTURE 143, 221

How can you honor God with your life? Deuteronomy 6:4-6; Psalm 119:33-40, 97-104; Micah 6:8; John 6:28, 29; Colossians 3:17

DRUG ADDICTION   50, 121

See Scriptures for disease.

EVANGELISM   65, 166, 178, 186

Sharing the good news of Jesus no matter the cost: Matthew 28:18-20; Acts 1:8; Acts 5:17-42; Acts 18:1-11

Explaining God's Word to others in a way that's easy for them to understand: *Philip and the Ethiopian*— Acts 8:26-39; *Paul in Athens*—Acts 17:16-34; *Priscilla and Aquila with Apollos*—Acts 18:18-28

FAITH   25, 202

A few examples of faith: *Rahab*—Joshua 2; Joshua 6:22, 23; Hebrews 11:31; *a Roman military officer*—Matthew 8:5-13; *children*—Luke 18:15-17

One gigantic list of people who had faith: Hebrews 11

FAMILY   14, 17, 36, 43, 56, 69, 94, 112,
153, 159, 208, 230, 233

The Bible is full of examples of different family dynamics and family conflicts. In times of frustration, take a moment to consider your spiritual family: Matthew 12:46-50; John 1:12, 13; 1 Timothy 5:1, 2

FORGIVENESS   17, 112

What Jesus taught about forgiveness: Matthew 6:14, 15; Matthew 18:21-35

An example of a huge fight and then someone forgiving: *Esau forgives his brother Jacob*—Genesis 25:24-34; Genesis 27; Genesis 32:1-21; Genesis 33

Examples of people being forgiven: Mark 2:1-12; Luke 7:36-50

SELF-IMAGE   23, 72, 78, 83, 100, 237

Feeling low? Moses didn't feel he was good enough either: Exodus 3:1—4:17

But feel great—humans (that includes you!) are made in the image of God: Genesis 1:26, 27; Genesis 2:7, 20-23; Psalm 139

And you are important and have a job to do: 1 Timothy 4:12

SERVICE   166, 169, 174, 178, 182, 186, 189, 193, 197

Examples of people who served others: *leaders who served widows*—Acts 6:1-6; *Dorcas helped the poor and made clothes*—Acts 9:36-42

How can you serve others? Consider your spiritual gifts: Romans 12:1-8; 1 Corinthians 12

SEX   131, 148, 216

Sex is good—in marriage! God created it for a husband and wife: Genesis 1:28; Genesis 2:24, 25

Some Scriptures about sex outside of marriage: *David and Bathsheba*—2 Samuel 11:1—12:25; 1 Corinthians 6:13, 18-20; Hebrews 13:4; Romans 1:24-32

TEACHERS, DEALING WITH   65

The need to respect authority: Romans 13:1-7; 1 Peter 2:13-17

Praying for people who are in authority: 1 Timothy 2:1-4

TEACHING CHILDREN   174, 193

Warnings for teachers to teach with integrity: Mark 9:42; James 3:1

TRUST   14, 97, 226

A few people who trusted that God had a plan:
Abraham—Genesis 22:1-19; *Caleb*—Numbers 13:1, 2,
26-33; Numbers 14:36-38; *Mary*—Luke 1:26-38

POETRY   21, 32, 42, 64, 76, 88, 111, 136, 157, 177,
184, 192, 206, 224, 250

True Stories of Teens on a Sacred Journey

ENCOUNTERS WITH GOD

Be part of
ENCOUNTERS WITH GOD,
The Sequel,
email your story to
encounter@standardpub.com

Compiled by Kelly Carr

Be the WAVE

Daring to Believe God and Embrace Your Destiny

Rob Hensser

It was a hot sticky afternoon in the dusty little village in Northern India. A small team of young Christians had just arrived to spend two weeks performing community service and sharing their faith. Soon after their arrival, a village leader confronted them.

"I forbid you to speak about Jesus in our village!"

Shocked, the team went back to their sweltering little room, gathered under the slow squeaking ceiling fan—and prayed. What should they do? They felt that God had called them to share with these people; they must obey a higher law. Being sensitive to the cultural differences they humbly served the community and waited for the right opportunities to share their faith. A few days later the village elder returned. This time he brought the police with him. They arrested the team on the spot and took them to a jail cell in an old tower-like building. Before locking the cell door the man coldly said to the frightened prisoners, "I told you not to speak of this Jesus. You will spend the night in this cell and tomorrow one of you will die. You have the night to decide who it will be."

As the man turned to leave, a member of the group timidly spoke up. With trembling voice he asked, "What would it take for you to believe in our God?"

Without a moment's pause the elder turned on his heel. "Rain," he answered. "We have not had rain in months. Our crops are failing and people are starving."

In that moment a balloon of faith welled up in the young team member. His scratchy voice betrayed his nervousness, "Tomorrow before

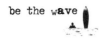

you return you will see rain, and it will be the tears of passion of our God for you."

"As you say," replied the elder, "but if not, *two* of you shall die and you will choose who." Then he slammed and bolted the heavy cell door.

The team was paralyzed with fear. In stunned silence they began to cry out to God in desperation. They prayed throughout the night. Hour after hour slipped away, and still they begged and pleaded with God. It was late into the night when one of the team felt God was giving them a word of encouragement from Mark 10:51. They turned to the passage and read the words of Jesus,

---

What do you want me to do for you? **Mark 10:51**

They were filled with a sense of anticipation as they cried out for rain. Faith slowly grew with dawn fast approaching. Praises and worship rose in their hearts until all glorified God in one voice. Whether it rained or not, they still would worship God . . . because he was worth it. Even if it meant giving their lives, they would trust the Father's will. Silence filled the cell as they waited, wondering when the man would return.

Out of nowhere there was a "plop" on the roof, then another followed by another. Dark clouds engulfed the clear skies. It was a torrential downpour.

"Friends!"

The voice seemed distant, drowned out by the rain, but there it was again, "Friends!"

Looking through the small barred window they could see the village elder down below. It had rained so much that he had to come by boat.

"Friends," he shouted out with tears streaming down his face. "I have come on the tears of passion of your God to worship him!"

Following God's will for our lives can seem so thrilling when we look back at having done it, but at the time it can be confusing and challenging. Many years before the birth of Jesus, a young girl experienced the thrill and challenge of finding the answers. Her name was Esther.

Esther ached with loneliness. Her parents had both died when she was very young. She sat by herself on a shaded wall watching other kids walk past hand in hand with their moms and dads. They looked so happy. The sweet smell of jasmine brushed her checks as a warm breeze slipped past. Esther took a deep breath, and then sighed. Why did God take both of her parents and leave her alone? She longed to have a normal family like the other kids, but she was forced to brave the world alone. The life of a street orphan was full of challenges and perils. It was a constant daily battle for survival. Cheat disease and you were forced to battle hunger. Overcome loneliness and you were confronted with violence. Not many kids lasted long on the cruel streets. The only hope was to join a gang of other un-wanted street kids to find shelter and protection in a makeshift family.

The challenge was even greater for a girl. Girls were weak and vul-nerable. Esther would not find acceptance or compassion from any of the young orphan boys. Where could she go, what could she do to es-cape? If someone did not step in on her behalf she would be doomed. Providentially, someone did. Esther didn't have to face the prospect of life on the streets. Her elder cousin Mordecai took her in. She wouldn't have to spend cold nights huddled for shelter in a dark alley, or scrounge through garbage for food. She was fortunate and she knew it, but she still longed for her own family. She missed her parents and yearned for her mother's embrace.

Esther held her small bag close to her chest, hugging it like a trusted teddy bear. She felt awkward as she followed her cousin up the stone stairs. She hardly knew him and now he was all the family she had in the world.

"Well, here we are," he said pushing open the simple wooden door.

Esther held her breath as she stepped into her new world. The house was small—just two rooms separated by a short beaded curtain. There was no furniture, just a couple of mats on either side of the room. A large pot filled with water sat in the corner. A piece of string hung from one wall to the next laden with clothes drying in the musty heat. During the day this room was the living room, dining room, kitchen and laundry. At night Mordecai hung a white sheet on the string dividing the room into bedrooms.

"This will be your side; you can keep your things in this wooden chest next to the mat. Just be sure to roll up your things each morning," he said, pointing to the small wooden box.

"Through that door are the toilet and a water jar for showering. If you prefer a bath I'm afraid you will have to go to the river."

Mordecai smiled awkwardly. He had no idea if young girls preferred to shower or bathe and now as he looked around he realized how sterile his home must look to her.

"Er, we can pick up a few things to make the place look a little more like home. If you want, you can come to the market tomorrow and help me choose." He smiled a vaguely confident smile. Esther relaxed and began to unload her bag into the chest. She liked her cousin, even if he was a bit odd.

Days turned into months and months into years.

"You get taller every day!" Mordecai joked, "Are those sandals already too small?"

Esther laughed, "There must be something in the water!"

She had grown to love her cousin. He was funny, loving and respected by everyone in the community. As the sun began to set Esther and Mordecai climbed the narrow stairs up to the roof where it would be cooler. They sat in the shade eating and looking over the ancient city of Susa, the capital of Persia. Many years before, her grandparents had been taken captive

by the Babylonians and forced to leave their home in Israel for a life of slavery in Babylon. The Babylonian Empire eventually fell to the mighty Persians. The Persians were not hard tyrants like their predecessors. The Jewish people were offered freedom and allowed to return home. But where was home? The older generation had all but died out. For the rest, this was home. Israel was a distant and precarious place and few returned. So like most of the Jewish people, Mordecai and Esther remained in Persia where Mordecai had a good job serving the king as a gatekeeper.

In many ways Esther was a lot like you and me. She dreamed of what the future would hold. Would she fall in love and have a family of her own? What would her husband be like? Would she be famous? What was God's will for her life? What was her destiny? How would she navigate the road of God's will for her life?

It was all over the news. Everyone was talking about it. The king of Persia was on the lookout for a new wife. Every corner shop was buzzing with the latest gossip. The king had decided to hold his very own beauty pageant. Young girls from all over Persia were being brought to the palace to compete.

"Esther, you've got mail," her cousin said, a little surprised, as he rummaged through the stack at breakfast.

Esther opened the letter and her heart froze. The hairs on the back of her neck stood stiff. Her mind started to swim. The last thing she remembered was a feeling of nausea overwhelming her and then everything went blank. She hit the ground like a sack of potatoes. Her head throbbed as she slowly opened her eyes. Mordecai was leaning over her with a damp cloth pressed to her forehead. Esther was overwhelmed with a feeling she had not known since she was a little girl sitting on a wall watching families. The letter was a summons to the palace. But how? Who had even noticed a shy, awkward orphan girl?

As she walked through the palace gates Esther felt confused and very nervous. What would happen to her? What did all this mean? When would she see her cousin again? Would she ever be allowed to return to her safe little home? What if the king wasn't pleased with her? Then again, what if he was? She was led into a large marble room. It was a comfortable room with lots of soft pillows and a fountain gently trickling in the middle. Tables were laden with sumptuous fruit and the finest vegetables. Esther's focus was on all the other young girls there with her. *There must be dozens of us here,* she thought aloud. Finally a gong sounded and a short fat man, who was well-dressed and seemed very self-important, waddled into the room. He cleared his throat loudly, then spoke, "For the next twelve months, this will be your new home. You must not leave. During this time you will be prepared to go before the king. Then he will decide."

Twelve months? I have to stay here a year? That's a lifetime! Esther felt sick to her stomach as waves of depression came over her. She longed to go home, back to the security of her cousin and her safe little life. For the next twelve months she would have to undergo beauty treatments, practice walking like a queen, and of course work on her talent! Should she sing or maybe dance? (Could you imagine taking a year to get ready to go out for an evening on the town?) When her turn came she would be presented to the king. If he liked what he saw, he would take her for his wife. She looked at the beautiful marble rooms, the richly appointed beds and the bathtubs! It was just like a fairytale—a common girl who became a princess.

Sound romantic? I doubt it. Esther had no choice in all this. Unlike other fairytales, Esther had not fallen in love with her Prince Charming. She hadn't even met him! He wasn't all that charming either. The king was not interested in winning her heart. He didn't pace the floor thinking of romantic schemes to overwhelm her with love and affection. He either liked what he saw or you spent the rest of your life locked in his harem knitting socks, hoping the phone might

ring. Esther had been ripped away from her life, family and friends—thrown into a new and strange world, where she no longer had any control over her decisions. All she had left was her trust in God. He was in control of her life, right? She had always believed that. Ever since being a poor orphan taken in by a kind relative, she had believed that God had a plan for her life. She swallowed, took a deep breath and decided to continue living her life as an offering to God.

Every day for twelve long months Esther gazed into the sky and thought of home. The walls were so high. All she had seen for months was the bright blue sky. She felt desperately lonely. Why was she even there? She looked around at the other girls primping and preparing. They all seemed prettier and more talented. Esther felt so empty. She even had to keep her faith hidden. The other girls just talked about all the shopping they could do with a royal charge card. It was tough, but she would trust and follow her heavenly Father. She continued to mark days, weeks and months off the calendar.

Finally, the big day arrived. The king summoned her to dinner. She was so nervous she could hardly eat a thing. The royal dining room was so big and the king was at the far end. Esther wondered if he could even see her. Where did all these people come from? She was dreading having to perform in front of this crowd. She rushed into her room and threw herself onto the bed. Burying her face in the soft feathery pillow she began to cry. She longed for her mom. Esther cried herself to sleep, partly as a release after one year of preparation, partly because she thought it had gone so horribly wrong. The king hardly seemed to look at her.

The next morning the short fat guy who was in charge of the beauty pageant announced, "The rest of the pageant is cancelled, the king has chosen . . . Esther!"

The months of hard work had paid off. The king was physically attracted to Esther—she was beautiful—but there was something else about this girl. She had a countenance, a depth, and she soon won royal favor and approval. God had raised Esther up from orphan to mother of a nation.

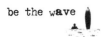

Every young girl dreams of being a princess, and Esther was no different. As a little girl her cousin would take her to see the beautiful palace and fountains. She would clutch his hand, close her eyes and dream of being a princess—to have beautiful clothes and sleep on a bed of soft luxurious cushions. Surely that was just a childish fantasy . . . she rubbed her eyes and pinched herself expecting to wake up any minute. It was real; she was princess of a mighty empire.

The wedding was like a bedtime story. Vibrant flowers overflowed in every room of the palace. The halls were rich with an aroma of the finest spices and draped in shimmering silks and flowing linen. Every citizen of Susa and people from all over the empire lined the streets to take in the event. The entire nation ground to a halt to tune in to the spectacle. Esther was the people's princess. A young common girl, one of them, was about to be crowned. People jostled in the streets as they lined up to wave their flags, hoping to catch a glimpse of her carriage as it passed. The deafening cheers and trumpet blasts moved along the crowd in pace with the carriage. Her long gown flowed behind her as her attendants entered and glided down the aisle. It was like a dream and every citizen of the empire was invited.

Esther didn't have long to adjust to her new life before its purpose became clear. Her position as queen was not simply by chance. God had a destiny for her to fulfill. Haman, a wicked advisor and close confidant to the king, felt threatened by Mordecai. Haman vowed to take his revenge by annihilating the entire Jewish population. Like a snake he deceptively slithered through the shadows of the palace laying his plan. Then, when the time was perfect, he deceived the king to write it as law. Nothing could stop the massacre now—nothing except the move of God. She didn't know it yet, but Esther was the only hope for her people.

BE THE WAVE, 02954
Order your copy now
by calling 1-800-543-1353
or by visiting www.standardpub.com

refuge \ˈre-fyüj\
shelter or protection from danger or distress

"My salvation and my honor come from God alone.
He is my refuge, a rock where no enemy can reach me.
O my people, trust in him at all times.
Pour out your heart to him,
for God is our refuge."
—Psalm 62: 7, 8, NLT

In the Old Testament God provided six "cities of refuge" where a person could seek safe haven from vengeance. These cities were places of protection. Today refuge™ will provide you the safe haven you need to grow in your relationship with God.

 www.rfgbooks.com